PAPA BOIS: KING OF PARADISE

By

ROSELLE THOMPSON

EAGLE PUBLICATIONS

Published by Eagle Publications

P O Box 73374, London W3 3FZ, England.
A Paperback Original

First published in the United Kingdom in 2022

Text copyright © 2022 Roselle Thompson

The right of Roselle Thompson to be identified as the Author of this work has been asserted by her.

ISBN 978-1-8381068-7-4

A CIP catalogue record for this book is available from the British Library
All Rights Reserved
This book is sold subject to the condition that it shall not, by way of trade or otherwise, be lent, hired out or otherwise circulated in any form of binding or cover other than that in which it is published. No part of this publication may be reproduced, stored in a retrieval system, or transmitted in any form or by any means (electronic, mechanical, photocopying, recording or otherwise) without the prior written permission of Eagle Publications.

All paper used by Eagle Publications is SFI (Sustainable Forestry Initiative) and PEFC (Programme for the Endorsement of Forest Certification Schemes) Certified.
This is a work of fiction. Names, characters, incidents and dialogues are products of the author's imagination or are used fictitiously. Any resemblance to actual people, living or dead, events or locales is entirely coincidental.

Printed in the United Kingdom and United States by Lightning Source for Eagle Publications

www.eaglepublications.org.uk

CONTENTS

Introduction	i-xxvii
Notes to the Introduction	xxviii-xxx
Characters	
PROLOGUE	1
ACT 1 SCENE 1: Welcome to Paradise!	3
ACT 1 SCENE 2: The Best Laid Schemes	10
ACT 1 SCENE 3: A Sense of Belonging	15
ACT 1 SCENE 4: A Musical Accolade	23
ACT 2 SCENE 1: Grief & Pain	31
ACT 2 SCENE 2: "Them-and-Us"	36
ACT 2 SCENE 3: Grave Concerns	43
ACT 2 SCENE 4: Gangsters & Greedy Men	51
ACT 2 SCENE 5: Schemes Go Awry	56
ACT 3 SCENE 1: The Dilemma!	60
ACT 3 SCENE 2: Making Supplications	69
ACT 3 SCENE 3: Massa Day Done!	75
ACT 3 SCENE 4: A Last Ditch Attempt	84
ACT 3 SCENE 5: 'The Best Laid Schemes…	90
ACT 3 SCENE 6: …Can go awry, and leaves us only grief and pain'	98
ACT 3 SCENE 7: As it was in the beginning……..	102
EPILOGUE	110
GLOSSARY	114

INTRODUCTION

This play, *Papa Bois: King of Paradise*, is a work of fiction, based on the Caribbean legendary character and folktale [1]**Papa Bois**. Although the tale originates from Africa, via slaves on plantations in the Caribbean, the name is a derivation of [2]*French Creole;* '*Papa,*' meaning 'father,' and '*Bois*', which is *Standard French* for 'woods or forest'. *Papa Bois* is one of the oldest Caribbean folklores, from islands such as Grenada, Trinidad and Tobago, Dominica, Martinique, and St. Lucia; islands with a French colonial history. *Papa Bois* is also known by other names, including *"Maitre Bois"* or 'Master of the woods, and *"Daddy Bouchon"* or 'hairy man.' According to Caribbean folklore, he is married to [3]*Mama Dlo*, also spelt *Mama D'Leau*, who is the protector and healer of all river animals.

      In this well-known Caribbean folktale, *Papa Bois* lives in the forest and is the 'Father or Protector of the animals' that live there. He is attributed sportsman-like qualities, because he can run faster than any creature. He is often seen by hunters and other people who live near the forest, and is said to rescue animals from snares and treats the sick ones in his dwelling. *Papa Bois* is also said to appear in different forms: as an old man who is very hairy like an animal and is usually only dressed in a pair of ragged trousers, with a bamboo horn hanging from his belt. When he takes the form of a human in old, ragged clothes, he is hairy and very old, or can appear as extremely strong and muscular; cloven hoofed, with leaves growing in his beard.
It is said that *Papa Bois* can be kind, but at the same time, can also be dangerous, when angry. He is known to cast spells on bad hunters and turn them into wild hogs. As the 'Guardian of all the animals,' *Papa Bois* sounds a cow's horn to warn them of approaching hunters. He neither tolerates killing for killing's sake, nor the wanton destruction of the forest. In fact, he is said to have the power of metamorphosis, and can appear as a deer, to observe hunters unnoticed, or lead men deep into the forest,

INTRODUCTION

then reveal his true self, to warn them. At times, he is known to vanish, leaving the hunters lost, or on a quest to comply with some form of punishment. There are many stories of *Papa Bois* appearing to hunters, and advice usually given is, if you should meet *Papa Bois*, you must be very polite, and greet him with, "*Bon jour, vieux Papa*" or "*Bon Matin, Maitre.*" If he stops to interact with you, be respectful and do not look at his feet!

As *Custodian of the trees* in the forests, *Papa Bois* requires men and women to uphold the traditional conservation measures; which is, he must be petitioned and appeased, along with the ancestors, with libation and prayers, before trees are cut down. In some areas in the Caribbean, before a [4]*Maroon* or cutting down forest areas for use, apart from pouring libation on the earth, money and flowers are also left, to show appreciation and respect. This conservation code stipulates that those cutting down trees, must cut only what is needed, and not a single tree more; to avoid wanton waste, disrespect or offend the ancestral spirits.

This method of valuing and showing respect to the land, has direct linkages with African metaphysical ontology. The timeline of the tales reaching the Caribbean would have commenced during the 16th century to mid-19th century. During this time, transplantation, acculturation, and synthesis of African cultures among the slaves in their new environment, created altered versions of African cultures that seemed more relevant in the new environment; hence variations in content, intent, and transmission in the region. Moreover, with its French name, the *Papa Bois* tale would have been transmitted by French-Creole speaking Africans, and French colonisers, living among the slaves on plantations in the Caribbean.

THE COLONIAL BACKGROUND

The background to colonisation in the *Papa Bois* folktale, began with Africans who were captured and traded on the African continent, and then shipped via the Transatlantic slave

INTRODUCTION

crossing, to work as slaves on plantations in the Caribbean; generally, from the 15th to the mid-19th century. It was a period that ended in rebellion, emancipation and post- emancipation periods of trading and development in the Caribbean. However, prior to colonisation, the Caribbean was populated by its own people – [5]Caribs, Arawaks and in some areas, Tainos; Amerindians from South America, from as early as 3600BC. These indigenous peoples had evolved their own civilisation, until the 1600's, when the British, Spanish, Dutch and French colonials arrived, which resulted in conflict among the indigenous peoples, in the region. It is widely known that many of the Caribs and Arawaks, throughout the Caribbean, resisted colonisation; some fought colonisers, other chose to either maim or kill themselves, rather than be caught and forced into slavery; thereby drastically depleting their numbers.

However, warfare continued during the 1600's between the British and Caribs and Arawaks within the region, and with later fierce pursuit and competition between other European countries, (French, Spanish and Dutch), for the Caribbean islands, colonisers conquered individual Caribbean islands at different times, and grew the region's economy by transporting African slaves and establishing the Slave Trade until 1834. Subsequently, the various waves of colonisers to the Caribbean, with their own administrators, mixed with the slave population, e.g., Yoruba, Igbos/Ibos, Congo, Ibibio, Akan and Malinke people; from West and Central Africa, became the largest ethnic group in the region; thus creating [6]*Creole* identity in the mixed environment.

The inter-mixing of these races and tribes with European colonialists, created offspring that were known as [7]*Mulattos;* a term used to describe people of mixed black and white ancestry. French input came from French settlers, who had also migrated within the Caribbean region, from the French Antilles, (since some of the islands were French colonies at the time) to work on sugar plantations.

INTRODUCTION

Later in 1834, with the abolition of slavery, a further influx of migrants; Indian indentured labourers, were brought in as cheap labour, with their own varieties of culture and languages intact. This group was followed by European indentured servants, including those of French, Spanish, Portuguese, British (*e.g. Irish, Scottish, and Welsh*); much later Chinese, Lebanese, Arab, Norwegian, and Mexican origins – all joined in the already culturally diverse environment; hence the resultant fusion of cultures in the Caribbean region.

THE FOREST AND AFRICAN TRADITIONAL THOUGHT

The folktale *Papa Bois*, is said to have originated from Africa, and transplanted in the Caribbean by slaves. Therefore, the existence of *Papa Bois* and many other African-derived folktales in the region, show that despite the hundreds of years of slavery, these tales have survived and have become part of the discourse and thinking in the Caribbean region. However, the importance of highlighting its linkages to the forest in African traditional thought, makes it inseparable from African ontology. In such discourse, there is a belief that society has a common bond with nature; without the duality of human versus non-human forms. It was believed that all forms, whether humans, animals, plants, the sea, and trees, are all interconnected and come from a Creator or God; on whom each one is dependent for its existence. Consequently, the dominant thought is a belief that all things are infused with the life-force of God. This view is confirmed by [8]Ehusani (1991), who states that the African sees the universe as one in which humans are at the centre, and is infused with a sacred mystical order that should not be disturbed. Hence, adherence to this African world-view, as discussed in Act 2 Sc. 3, shows a Caribbean adaptation of such thinking; namely, the customary practice that individuals must seek permission to 'disturb.' In this Caribbean folktale, the permission needed is appeasement of the deity *Papa Bois*, with an offering or libation. Conversely, in this Play Dennis Palmer,

INTRODUCTION

the protagonist, shows a lack of understanding of this knowledge, by treating the folklore with contempt and derision; for which he suffers the consequences, at the end of the play.

Notwithstanding Dennis' perspective, what is also suggested in this Play, is that such practices inform a very early and continuing conservationist and environmentally conscious attitude towards nature, beginning with African slaves, in their New World (Caribbean) environment; long before 21st century's global concerns about climate change became vogue. It also confirms that despite colonisation, and the incursion of globalisation, there are still vestiges of this traditional African thought in the Caribbean region. These are perpetuated via the *Papa Bois* folktale, and is evident in the belief that the forested landscape is seen as a sacred place, that is inhabited by super-human forces. This is intimated when Isaac states;

> *It's like runnin' Papa Bois away from the land, after all these past generations upon generations, we been followin' the tradition without trouble.* (Act 2 Sc. 3)

In traditional African thought and practice, the forest was seen as, not only important to human life, but also important for non-human species, which depended on its environment for survival. These include animals, other living organisms, resources for food, for building, recreation and other ecological importance. Examples are, regulating temperature, preventing soil erosion - all which help to ameliorate the crises caused by climate change concerns today. Such a view is suggested in this Play, as being rooted in African pantheistic and metaphysical ontology; that the forest has an active force or spirit that gives it communal value and life.

Ultimately, *Papa Bois: King of Paradise* projects the view that the land, such as Dennis Palmer's 10-acre *Paradise Estate*, is of great value in the community, and in the wider context of a traditional world view. Consequently, this Play presents the protagonist's hubris and hamartia, as the cause of

INTRODUCTION

his downfall, because he lacked an understanding of the interdependence and co-existence of both humans and non-humans alike in the community. This overriding concern is embodied in the fact that an environment, without its natural landscape and beauty of trees or forests, used for goals that have no positive, lasting effect environmentally or communally; eventually harms human and natural health. This is echoed in the discussions in (Act 3 Sc. 1) that, clearing the ten acres of land of all its trees, shrubs, and non-human life-forms, in favour of planting and cultivating marijuana for quick personal profits, is a measure that falls short of sustaining life for present and future generations. This is voiced by Moses who states:

> *"You see, the land is the soul and heart-beat of a country, and the birth-right of its people, especially the young."* (Act 1 Sc. 1)

Dennis' mother also understood the importance of the land she intends to purchase, when she says,

> *"... it has plenty cocoa and nutmeg, with enough space to propagate all kinds of produce to live off the land."* (Act I Sc. 1).

Additionally, embodied in the discussions voiced about the misuse of the natural landscape, is also concern about the destruction of the essential functioning of the land; absorbing carbon dioxide and producing oxygen for human survival, as well as habitats for its non-human life forms.

The protagonist, this Play shows, tried to alter the prevailing, traditional African world view, in favour of his greed, and neo-colonialist ideology; that of commoditising the natural landscape for his own short-term, selfish monetary goals; without political objection. Therefore, *Papa Bois* as a Play, seems to confirm the view that wanton destruction of the land merits reclamation by both the villagers and *Papa Bois*. It can also be seen symbolically, as reclamation of the traditional

INTRODUCTION

African world-view about the forest or landscape; or at least recapturing African spirituality, that realistically presents a model to combat current global climate change and help to sustain human life. An over-riding suggestion in this Play, is that humans' role is to use the Creator's elemental creations moderately, for sustenance, whilst simultaneously, and compulsorily, conserving them. Such actions are expedient in our 21st century; due to present and future consequences about global warming, and climate change threats to humanity.

THE CARIBBEAN STORYTELLING TRADITION

The *Papa Bois* folktale, like all other Caribbean folktales, were orally transmitted beliefs, myths, and tales from one generation to another, originating (though not exclusively) from Africa, told by the slaves who were brought to the region. The folk tales were mainly about beliefs, myths, and practices of African-Caribbean people. This is why some tales have religious figures or supernatural folklore figures, which possess characteristics that are identical to those of African deities. But, this body of African folklore has been synthesised and influenced by English, French and to a lesser degree, Spanish and Dutch colonisers, who brought their own brand of lore into the Caribbean region. These different types of folklore found expression in the Caribbean, seen as the *new* environment, were later used in situations that warranted use of a tale as a kind of coded message; such as in situations that needed instilling caution, warning, applying cunning, courage, or good sense. Subsequently, these tales which were fused with African lore, had a new function and expression in the Caribbean environment.

The existence of Caribbean folktales shows how, over the hundreds of years of slavery, these tales have been indelibly etched in the subconscious of the Caribbean people, so that transmitting the stories from one generation to the other, symbolises the transference of a kind of Caribbean cultural

INTRODUCTION

heirloom. It is for these reasons that these stories find expressions within the Caribbean landscape, and evidence a fusion of Africa's deep consciousness within the people's psyche, through their recreated lore. These tales have generally been kept alive by the older generation; those who have transmitted them to surviving groups of younger Caribbean people. But with the passage of time, as well as that of the older generation, many have ceased the practice of the traditional storytelling.

This tradition with which the old folks have grown up, is an age-old experience. These [9]*"crick-crack!"* story-telling sessions would usually be conducted on a warm moonlit night, in a Caribbean village, as crickets and fireflies dance in the tropical air. Under a large tree in someone's yard, eager village children would gather for a folk event. The nearby trees, casting giant shadows around them, create a mood of togetherness, mystery, contained fear, and camaraderie. Everyone is seated on the ground, in a semi-circle and a Caribbean folktale, from one of the old folks, is told to the delight and live participation of its expectant audience.

However, in modern times, the traditional mode of transmission, the images of the folks and the physical story-telling sessions, have diminished. This dilemma, has been blamed on succeeding generations of Caribbean youths, both in the region and abroad, who seem to have lost touch with this once vibrant traditional experience and are no longer passing on the tradition. Others blame the changing landscape and the profusion of bright electric lighting everywhere; which has robbed the landscape of the story-telling aura of darkness, moonlight, and mysterious night shadows. In fact, many Caribbean youths (especially those born in the Diaspora), are somewhat oblivious of the very existence of the language, lore, and stories of the Caribbean past. Consequently, it is my belief that a Caribbean Writer's role includes preserving the tales and their essence in Caribbean culture, as well as their meaning in

INTRODUCTION

Caribbean people's lives, in whatever format seems relevant in our present time.

LANGUAGE ISSUES IN THE PLAY

(a). The Writer's dilemma

Since preservation and perpetuation of the tales is necessary, the issues relating to how, and in what manner, should the Caribbean writer use language to present his writing, is a long debated one; stemming largely from the 1930's emergence of a Caribbean written tradition. The dilemma faced by the early writers, which is somewhat relatable today, centres on the pros and cons of using Standard English; non-Standard forms e.g., dialect, and Creolised forms of speech, or a mixture of all - to present their work. Early Caribbean writing shows that an individual writer's choice of medium was based on their targeted audiences, therefore Standard English was used. Reasons proffered were that using the non-standard English forms meant that the work would be limited to a parochial audience, despite their greater understanding of the Creole language varieties.

Therefore, the choice of using Standard English, to gain a wider audience, meant losing the "authenticity" of voices and speech varieties that aid meaning in context, within the text. This is because the written Standard English form tended not to fully represent the "voice" of the folks. Added to this dilemma was the fact that publishers of Caribbean writings, were based outside of the Caribbean, e.g., London and USA, and their decisions to publish a writer's work, influenced by strict adherence to Western conventional writing forms, meant they imposed restrictions on the non-Standard forms being used. Either way, the Caribbean writers' constriction meant that they were not "free" to write as they pleased. However, since the mid-20th century, though writers have overcome much of the earlier restrictions, some are still faced with the dilemma of

INTRODUCTION

whether to maintain characteristic features of the Creolised spoken varieties, to convey a sense of Caribbean identity within the canon; (since it enables some representation of nuances, and localised meanings); whilst others choose to modify the language, in order to appeal to both Standard English and non-Standard English speakers alike.

What is undisputed, is that the Caribbean does have a polylingual environment which stems from its racially mixed background. This has already been discussed above as stemming from slavery and colonisation, by a mixture of English, Dutch, French, and Spanish settlers, who were white, and to a much larger extent, West African slaves, indentured Indian labourers, and much later, other settlers. Slaves, being the larger percentage of the population, came predominantly from three West African areas: in the 17th century from Senegal to Sierra Leone, from Liberia to Nigeria in the 18th century and in the last period of slavery from Angola. Each African area consisted of their own tribal groups. The British colonial administration consisted of people from different parts of the UK, i.e., Scotland, Wales, or Ireland, and each with their own brand of colloquial and regional dialects. Added to this linguistically mixed situation in 1800, were the indigenous Amerindian languages, which created a fusion or synthesis of languages in the Caribbean environment. Therefore, far from being one Caribbean language, there were several permutations of speech that created what is recognised as a Creole language. A Creole language is identified by its combination of African syntax and European lexicon/words. This development of the Creole language was confirmed by [10]J.J. Thomas, who identified the Creole language as *"a dialect framed by Africans from a European tongue."* Today, Scholars agree that the written forms of the English language, in the former and current British-controlled Caribbean countries, conform to the spelling and the grammatical styles of Britain.

INTRODUCTION

However, although there is an acknowledgement of Standard English, as the official form of communication, in most English-speaking Caribbean islands, there are islands whose history evidence exchanges of European domination, so that one island may have more than one Western language spoken in its environment. Caribbean countries where this has occurred, show that over time, fused with other varieties as already stated, have a unique style of speaking and writing; resulted in both *English Creole* and *French Creole* languages.

The French-based language has had less officially enforced means of communication, compared to the British Standard English; due to the shorter time the French colonials ruled in the region. Notwithstanding this, vestiges of French are still used by the older generation; as represented by the Title of this Play – ***Papa Bois***. The Creole varieties are also identified in some utterances among the older folks, popularly called *patois* (pronounced *pat-wa*), regarded as a "dying" language which is stylized, but is becoming an anomaly in the modern environment. These factors relate to the changing ways of life, influenced by globalisation, as well as other *external* factors; such as migration to metropolitan cities, and the necessity of Standard English usage for all official communication – media platforms, legal institutions, and education. Added to these are *internal* factors, which have influenced the language of the people, such as migration within the islands of the Caribbean region. The latter has resulted in strong similarities in vocabulary, syntax, and morphology, between Caribbean islands.

(b). The Polylingual Environment

We can agree that given the forced contact of outsiders into the Caribbean region onto the indigenous Amerindians, their language was impacted on by varieties of spoken languages of the slaves from West and Central Africa. Many of these slaves

INTRODUCTION

were literate in their own native languages and not being from one single area in Africa, spoke different tribal dialects, were forced to speak the European colonisers' languages, in the region.

Therefore, it is important to note that the Caribbean varieties evolved out of the necessity to communicate in a common language for survival on the plantations. Consequently, individual islands within the whole region, tend to have a European language dominance, due to the influence of their ruling colonial power, over periods of time. Historically, colonisers had fought for control of individual islands; seizing, and losing them at different times, so that their diverse histories are also reflected in the spoken languages of the people.

Additionally, when Mikey (Act 3 Sc 1), mentions the emerging Chinese influence in the region, there is a sense that he is alluding to the additional cultures that continue to impact on the already mixed environment in the Caribbean. Varieties of utterance can be based on the age of the person speaking, and whether that person received formal education. Added to this is the fact that the Creole languages, over 500 years old, have been wrongly classified as dialects of English and French. Co-existing as it does alongside Standard English, Caribbean language varieties have been stigmatised because they are linked to slavery, poverty, backwardness, or lack of education, and those on the lower socio-economic levels in society.

In fact, this issue presented in Caribbean works of art, over the past 90 years, has been the subject of debates among scholars and writers within and outside of the region, who have debated whether to use Standard English for ease of access to a wider, global audience, or in limiting this to a parochial audience, insist on endorsing the legitimacy of Creole varieties in their texts. Similarly, it is hoped that the issue of language presented in this play will add to current debates, whilst highlighting the ability and skilfulness of Caribbean speakers to switch between Creole and Standard English, (or somewhere

INTRODUCTION

between the two), as well as other developed forms of expressions. Consequently, it adds to debates on Caribbean languages' right to be identified, recognised, and studied as Standard forms, and not as dialects of other languages.

(c). Characteristic Features of the Creole Language

It is important to note that orthography (spelling) of the Creole languages vary greatly, within Caribbean islands, since some choose to spell them phonetically e.g., *cyan,* for (can't); *kudnt,* for (couldn't); *whey* for (where), *mi* for *me*, and *seh* for *say*. The variety of Creolised spelling is most noticeable from island to island in proverbial sayings. As far as *Papa Bois: King of Paradise* is concerned, the importance attached to the Creole language, is its marked difference from Standard English. This is highlighted to draw attention to aspects of the language in the island/region. Here are some characteristic features of the **Creole language** used within this Play.

1. There is **no nasalisation at the end of words**, and **Consonant changes** – the *g* in present continuous verb tenses, are also common. particularly when it's used to present participle of verbs e.g., *everything, offering, disrespecting, turning*: Instead, these are used: *everythin', offerin', disrespectin' turnin',* (Act 2 Sc 3), (Act 3 Sc 1), (Act 3   Sc 3). Or *"It's like runnin' Papa Bois away."* And *"...it's openly disrespectin' our culture."* (Act 3 Sc 2)

2. **Creole English does not have the [nt] cluster** at the end of negative contracted forms, such as *can't, don't couldn't*. Instead, these forms are used: *cyan, doh,* (Act 4 Sc 3) e.g. *"He cyan come here and do that!"* or *"You cyan cut down the trees"* and *Ah doh need to tell all-you about the legend."* (Act 3 Sc. 2)

INTRODUCTION

3. The **dental aspirate is omitted in words** such as: *the, this, them, they, that*. Instead, these phonetic forms are used: *de, dis, dey/deh, dem* and *dat,* e.g. *"*Dat Dennis is not a real fiyah man." (Act 2 Sc 3)

4. **Different sets of pronouns** are used to highlight a Caribbean utterance e.g. *mi* or *meh* for me; *ah* for I; *dem* for them; *deh/dey* for they; *dat* for that; *dis* for this; *wi* for we.

5. The common **use of the first pronoun *I*, which is often replaced by *ah*, and a specific form uttered by Rastafarians,** *I'n'I,* used to mean the collective "we"; in other words, meaning, *brothers and sisters or brethren.* The choice of using *ah* or *I*, among the characters, depends on the state of emotions presented. Used interchangeably, it creates emphasis in speech. For example, the sentence, *I don't know*, is presented as *"Ah doh know,"* or *"Morning Miss V, ah got a registered letter for you today.* (Act 1 Sc 2). Both forms *I* and *ah*, can also be used by an individual in one sentence utterance, for different emphasis.

6. **Word order is often reversed**, so that instead of saying *all of you*, is presented as *"all-you."* For example, *"Let me start or little gathering by thanking all-you for coming."* (Act 2 Sc 3). In presenting American urban talk, the form suggested here, is *"you-all"* or *"y'all."* Valeria in Act 1 Sc. 3 says, *"Mmm! I'm having the best time ever, you-all."*

7. **Omission of verbs** is common in **Creole English**, so that what is heard is, *"Lots of them up in your area?"* Instead of, *"Are there lots of them in your area?"* In Act 2 Sc 1, Ashley asks Viola, *"Okay, so what she saying now? Or*

INTRODUCTION

"He already bought all kinds of equipment from America. (Act 2 Sc3)

8. In most cases, Creole English **omits the third person singular** (s) at the end of verbs. Example: *"He plan to marry her."* Instead of, *"He plans to marry her."* Or (Act 2 Sc 5), *"He also plan to build a hotel complex."* (Act 2 Sc3)

9. **Repetition is used to convey emphasis or a sense of immediacy**. For example, "Is 'fraid, they 'fraid of revenge. But I'm not afraid though!" (Act 3 Sc 3). Put in another form the word is repeated in quick succession: e.g. Dat likky-likky bwoy, im too feisty! (A3 Sc7) or as Mikey says, "We must claim our voice back and speak loud-loud, about what's happening." Act 3 Sc1).

10. **Different uses of pronouns to reflect a Creolised pattern of speech** e.g. *mi* = me; *dem* = them and *leh* = let. *"Come leh we read it man."* Or *"Ah couldn' expect better."* (Act 1 Sc 2)

11. Use of **double negatives** in sentences, e.g. *"No, ah doh want no trouble, eh!"* (Act 2 Sc 2)

12. **Omission of past tense verbs** e.g. *"I get letter from America."* Or *"Okay, so when they coming back?"* (Act 1 Sc 3)

13. A noticeable feature of the Caribbean region's linguistic background is the **language fusion** that has taken place in both **French-based** and **English-based Creole varieties**. Both are referred to as *patois*, pronounced *pat-wa*, e.g., **French patois** or **English patois** with the following features:

INTRODUCTION

A sentence or phrase can begin in one language and end with another, as in the title of the folktale e.g. *Papa Bois."* The word *"Papa"* is French-Creole for father, and the word *"Bois"* is standard French for *"Wood."* Similarly, the term, *"Papa God/Gawd,"* is an endearing term for *"Father God."* Also Moses explains the locals use of French Creole. "Well, we the old folks say it in French Creole, *J'ouvert,* means *fore day morning,* as we say in local parlance, but for you, I would just say, *day break*." (Act 1 Sc. 1.)

14. **There is also an input of Rastafarian language** in this Play, as represented by Egbert, speaking on behalf of the Rastafarian community in the island. Known as *"Iyaric,"* this language emerged from the late 1930s onwards, as a means of rejecting Standard English and the English culture's dominance on the psyche of the black man; in order to "rebuild an autonomous, black identity. In challenging the Anglophile culture, Rastafarians insisted on a language that reflected solidarity, self-reliance and Africanness."[11] The Rastafarian language is also referred to as *Rasta or dread talk*, and it's orthography shows a modification or mixture of both Standard English and Jamaican Creole.

In this Play *Papa Bois: King of Paradise, Azacca*'s speech exemplifies this Caribbean variety, when he shows solidarity with the revolutionaries planning to oust Dennis Palmer, and his colonial ideologies from the island. Azacca states, *"But hear noh, a lat a greedy betrayer 'tween us, jus' sittin pon dem backside saying mi nuh hav nutten fi complain bout, mi life irie, but mek ah tell you sumthin', I'n'I come here to say, jus' like Bob Marley did, wi guh chase dat crazy ballhead outta*

INTRODUCTION

town." (Act 3 Sc 3). *(See Glossary for translation and more explanation)*

15. Another factor of importance is that **Caribbean writers generally present the Creolised languages as they are expressed in their own individual islands.** For example, islands such as Martinique, Guadeloupe, Grenada, and Dominica, where French colonials dominated or still do today, continue to speak French, as an official language *(Martinique and Guadeloupe are still French colonies).* However, attempts have been made to create a Caribbean regional orthography, as seen in the various editions of [12]Richard Allsopp's *Dictionary of Caribbean English Usage.*

16. In addition, there are **other suggested standards of orthography and pronunciation across various islands;** all which attest to a movement away from the strictures of the inherited Standard Western forms of language and speech. Such movements are attempts to give primacy to the localised versions of Caribbean speech, as well as individual language identities within the region. The flourish of individual island language dictionaries, now accessible globally, also evidence this growing phenomenon.[13] However, in *Papa Bois: King of Paradise,* despite the characteristic features of Creole languages presented, there is also an attempt to modify the presentation of both the Creole and Standard English formations used. Strategies included in this Play are as follows:

    a. **Adapting some of the Creole forms**, especially omitting the *"g"* in present continuous verb tenses, such as, *goin',* use of the utterance *"eh"* and other characteristic features, as outlined

INTRODUCTION

above. These are represented in the language of the Barber Shop occupants, who symbolically present the speech of the older generation.

b. **Choosing to maintain some of the Standard English forms**, to make it easily accessible to purely Standard English readers, globally.

c. **Characters revert to Creole English,** as the natural vernacular, especially when displaying emotions or communicating in informal settings.

d. **Subtle distinctions in the varieties of language used**, are often shown between older generation characters (e.g., the different Barber Shop characters, the women in the church service) and the younger Caribbean speakers. For example, I allowed the formally educated characters to use a greater content of Standard English e.g., the Elders, Ashley (the retired teacher) and his wife Viola, the Reverend Truman, Dennis Palmer, and his workers. The revolutionaries were presented with Creolised speech patterns.

These strategies have been used to ensure that a kind of middle-ground is achieved, so as not to limit its global reach, or identification as a Caribbean Play, but firmly establish its existence within the Caribbean canon.

MIGRATION & RESETTLEMENT: CENTRAL THEMES IN THE PLAY

The Play's timeline is located in the late 20th century, commencing with the migration of Caribbean people, (the

INTRODUCTION

Palmers), to America in the early 1970's. As economic migrants, they left the Caribbean to seek employment, self-improvement, and financial maintenance of families back-home, in the Caribbean; factors which highlight a multitude of thematic concerns in the Play. For example, migration is voiced thus:

> **ASHLEY:** *"It's true, look how all man, Jack, and their brother, leave this country, running away with great speed, like a ball. And what happen in the long run? They rebound and bounce right back here – back to where? Home!" (Act 1 Sc 2)*

However, the Central theme of this play alludes to sentiments expressed in a poem by the Scottish Poet, [14]Robert Burns, which states, *"the best laid schemes of mice and men go oft awry and leave us only grief and pain."* Written in Scottish dialect, the poem is about a field mouse which happily builds his winter nest in a wheatfield, only for it to be destroyed by a ploughman. Consequently, the mouse which had dreamt of a safe, warm, winter, is now faced with the harsh reality of the wintry weather; loneliness and possibly death.

This allusion is highlighted in *Papa Bois: King of Paradise*, because the Play's scenarios reflect similar, migrant Caribbean nationals' decisions to emigrate and the repercussions of such actions. They live and work in the Diaspora, and subsequently purchase land and other possessions, with the hope and plan to either return, retire, relocate, or set up businesses in their *back-home*, for their future upkeep. However, the reality is, sometimes the accumulated wealth may never be enjoyed as expected or planned, because in the intervening period, despite careful planning, some Caribbean nationals may become incapacitated, die, or have their dreams curtailed or unfulfilled in some way.

Similarly, in this play, the Caribbean migrants', (the Palmers), demise in a road accident in New York, leaves their only son, Dennis, in *"grief and pain"* and this consequently led

INTRODUCTION

to both theirs and their son's failed dreams. The main reason is, Dennis is forced to forgo his own dreams in the American music industry, where he is a rising star, in order to locate in the Caribbean, (a place he once called *"backward,"* despite never having gone there), to claim his legacy – a mansion and a 10-acre estate. However, having lost both parents at once, the impact of their sudden demise on him, and his future plans, cause *'grief and pain,'* displayed as extreme personality transformations; mainly of a self-destructive nature. Dennis' plans and actions in the Caribbean subsequently clash with the locals; legally, culturally, spiritually, morally, and religiously. This leads to other inter-locking themes within the Play, such as loneliness, political ineptitude, neo-colonialism, corruption, poverty, conservation issues, making choices and unfulfilled dreams.

MIGRATION

The theme of migration or the need for Caribbean nationals to exit their islands, has been a direct response to economic problems since the nineteenth century. Due to the islands' colonial history of plunder and the economic impact of imperialism; a situation which affected the majority of individual islands in the region, the specific Caribbean location in this *Papa Bois* play has been purposely left unnamed. This is to draw attention to the symbolic nature of the drama and the prevalence of the issues portrayed, which can be applicable to individual islands within the region.

Up until 1965, the United States had openly discriminated against some nationalities, in favour of north western Europeans; making it difficult for migration from regions such as the Caribbean to their shores. However, the US Immigration Act of 1965, brought in a less biased approach, and this facilitated immigration from the new independent islands from the Caribbean to the USA. The greatest *"pull"* factors from the region, were the employment opportunities available

INTRODUCTION

abroad, where Caribbean citizens could resettle, and make a living to support those left behind at home.

In the play *Papa Bois,* the protagonist's Caribbean immigrant parents in Act 1 Sc2, discussed their emigration to the USA around the early 1970's, for economic reasons. In fact, from the mid-20th century, there has been an exodus of Caribbean people to places such as England, Canada, and the United States. Today, Caribbean immigrants live in large numbers in cities such as New York, Miami, Philadelphia, Boston, and London. During the late 1960's early 1970's, immigrant-Caribbean women were located in the nursing profession; working in hospitals and health-care institutions. Unlike England, where the majority of early Caribbean immigrants were males, in America, the post-1965 immigration period was dominated by female migrants; often joining their male counterparts or other family members.

A major *"push"* factor of migration was the expectation that remittances will be sent back home, to provide education, food, shelter, and medicines for loved ones. A reason for that *"push"* factor, was due to the depleted domestic economy; hence the importance of remittances from immigrants abroad, sustaining many Caribbean societies. However, this resulted in another factor; that of a "brain drain" of Caribbeans leaving the region, to settle in the Diaspora; as reported in a study conducted by the [15]United Nations in 2003. Therefore, whilst Caribbean societies gained economically from foreign remittances, they suffered real losses to these strong metropolitan cities, of some of the brightest and best "brains" from their countries.

Today, problems still exist where there are distinct ethnic groups, and class divisions, (some stemming from colonialism in the region); evident by the disparities amongst those who have material wealth, and those who are very poor. In *Papa Bois: King of Paradise*, some of the economic differences are marked by similar types of class divisions. Therefore, some of the resentment towards returning

INTRODUCTION

Caribbean nationals, can be traced to poverty, lack of opportunities, and the emergence of a social class formed by wealthy Caribbean migrants returning to the region. In other words, the emergence of a Caribbean middle class, or in some cases, a new Caribbean upper class. Ashley Palmer tries to explain to his nephew Dennis, the contesting views about 'newcomers' to the island thus:

> "They come here and try to pull rank over the natives, by showing off on them, and acting like colonial masters, all over again. So, the people here think, 'Who the hell they think they are?' " (Act 2 Sc. 2)

Consequently, underpinning this dichotomy, is the fact that it could encourage high crime rates in all forms; like the protagonist, Dennis Palmer, who entered the region with a drug-trading enterprise that could destabilise fragile economies; which he projected as an alternative, viable, economy, among the poor citizens. In such situations, Caribbean Leaders could be faced with difficulties, when deciding whether to fight crime with limited resources, and forego providing health care and education or, without action, become inundated with the illegal activities, that make them impotent to take preventative measures against such financially untenable activities.

In *Papa Bois: King of Paradise*, Dennis Palmer is shown to take advantage of people's poverty, by luring the young, old, and even government officials, with his lucrative drug-producing trade, and the visibility and ease of gaining ready-made cash from it. Therefore, the interlocking themes of corruption, political ineptitude among cash-strapped government officials, intimates that Caribbean societies could face real dangers from globalization. Also, given its strategic geographical position between South and North America, where illicit drugs - especially cocaine, are produced, consumed and traded, makes the Caribbean susceptible to competition from major drug-

INTRODUCTION

dealers; whose activities involve violence, and ruining lives from consumption of the drugs, as discussed in Act 3 Sc. 1. Consequently, the revolutionary zeal, and counter-attack, based on an island-wide concerted approach from the islanders, is projected as a way of tactically dealing with these problems; at a grass-roots level.

THE AMERICAN DREAM IN THE PLAY

Within the central theme of migration in the Play, is also a dominant dream theme; *the [16]American Dream*. The protagonist's Caribbean immigrant mother's decision to buy land in the Caribbean, is embodied in this Dream principle;

> *"...I know we are lucky to be in steady, employment, so we can save and carry out our long-term goals for returning home; y'know, our 'American Dream' in the Caribbean! (laugh). So right now, we really want to beat the iron while it's still hot."* (Act 1 Sc. 1.).

Even the Palmers' Italian neighbours - Matteo, Valeria, and their American-born son Gino - have a similar perspective; having also bought their own home in America. Like the Palmers, the Italian family had pursued their goals and achieved their *American Dream* which Matteo confirms as follows:

> *"Look at us today, at least we have something to show for it, our own American dream!"* (Act 1 Sc. 3).

The principle of the *American Dream* is based on the driving force of pursuing material wealth and the fruits of prosperity; seen in Dennis' parents' emigration to the USA, and a competing reality for immigrants and their children generally. The latter, many of whom are born in America, live a version of the *American dream* themselves. Thus, the ethos of living the *American dream* tend to clash with those outside of the experience of such 'dreams.' Dennis projects a version of the *American Dream* and believes he has an *"inalienable right"* in

INTRODUCTION

the Caribbean, to monopolise, a national enterprise of marijuana production, in his 10-acre estate; where he is subsequently daubed *King of Paradise*. His actions led to widespread condemnation, local objection, rioting and a concluding violent revolution. This hastens his demise and fortunes, seen as a failed dream, at the end of the play, as foreshadowed by allusion to Burn's poem.

The failure of another *American Dream* is seen in Dennis' Caribbean migrant parents' demise. Whilst living in America, they buy 10 acres of land and build a mansion on it, in the Caribbean, where they hope to retire. However, they later die in a car crash, close to their American exit-date. Despite their careful advanced planning for their future, they never got to completely fulfil or enjoy their 'dream.' Prior to their deaths, and not wishing to force their only son to join them on holidays, they had journeyed back and forth from the Caribbean to the USA, with their envisioned plans; to ensure their transacted assets were secure. They believed that one day Dennis would somehow acquiesce, and eventually settle with them in the Caribbean.

However, Dennis' past responses to all his parents invitations to jointly visit the Caribbean, were mostly met with derision, rejection, and a general negative mindset about the place being "*backward.*"

> "*Dad, I just know the Caribbean isn't ready for me yet. I think they haven't caught up with 20th century pace of life. And as for technology, to me, that place is bereft of real life and technological advancement.*" (Act 1 Sc. 3).

Dramatic irony is shown later, when he ends up inheriting their 10-acre Caribbean estate. Dennis is young, American-born, and a musician, who was making inroads into the music industry; having won the coveted **Best Newcomer in Music Award**. This early success made him a rising star in America, but

INTRODUCTION

unfortunately, once family tragedy struck, his own future plans in the industry were, like his parents, abruptly curtailed. Becoming the owner of their small Caribbean fortune, Dennis relinquished his ideas about music and instead, migrated to the Caribbean to claim his legacy.

One of the dramatic functions of the play is to augment our sense of the paradoxical complexity of Dennis Palmer's character. Initially, he is a happy young man, within a loving family, who has a clear vision of his future career and the potential to succeed. Later, this contrasts greatly, after he is bereaved, with the ensuing disillusions and outrageous conflicts he has with those in his adopted "homeland."

Dennis Palmer is a tragic hero, who is driven by his over-arching ambition to conduct an illegal drug trade; is passionate in his arguments, and easily sways those who are against his ideas. However, he becomes a murderous, and defiant villain, who submits to his greedy impulses; despite the overwhelming odds against him from the islanders. Dennis' turpitude is obvious, and this blinds him to his doomed situation, so that he responds with grit and stoicism throughout the play. However, it is not until the very end of the play, when he faces a gun at the point of his demise, that he realises he is truly powerless. Clearly, he is not Macbeth, who would fight to the end, 'till from my bones my flesh be hacked.' [17] Instead, Dennis begs pitifully, repeatedly, for his life.

> *Look guys, I know you're real mad right now,*
> *but we can still work something out.*
> *Ask me for anything you want.*
> *Please, I can give you whatever you want, just name it!*
> *(voice becomes louder) But whatever you do,*
> *please don't pull that trigger!* (Act Sc. 6)

In fact, the final image of Dennis as a vulnerable, frightened man, trapped in his bed, naked, and without his lackeys to

INTRODUCTION

defend him, is offset by the moral course of the plot. At the end, Dennis is without honour or friends, and theologically, it marks a sense of judgement for his descent into mortal sin, despair, for the direct, as well as indirect murders, of those his drug trading enterprise had impacted on. His earlier arrogance had caused him to posit the view that it was easy to achieve his *American Dream* in the Caribbean, with the presumptuous transformations he had visualised for the island. This ranged from importing technological advancement, and his own manpower into the island, to create new infrastructures for his benefit; controlling information by coercion and political bribery, especially those who attempted to counter his operations; influencing the state of the economy by flooding citizens with cash and drugs, facilitated by notorious drug-lords; were attempts to change the financial and cultural values of Caribbean demographics. Dennis' condescending attitude to the place is shown when he scoffs at the locals' traditional world view:

> *Hah! Papa Bois, indeed! STUPES! (sucks his teeth) That's just old folks stories and tales about backwardness from plantation life. We're in the 20th century, and as far as I'm concerned, we have to move with the times. (Act 2 Sc2)*

Consequently, based on his attitude above, both his hubris and hamartia hastened the failure of his dream, and his subsequent demise, as satire for the rising consumer materialism in society; seen in the chase for both Dennis' and his parents' *American Dream*. Rev Truman's perspective on the issues sums up the dilemma:

> *You see what I'm saying, they come over from their big overseas cities abroad, and think they better than us – bringing in their foreign ideas here and trying to tell us ours is backward! I say it's them who's backward, not*

INTRODUCTION

> *us, for not understanding our folk culture, traditions, peoples way of life, and our history!* (Act 2 Sc. 3)

The irony of this Play's plot is Dennis' misplaced belief, that he was the *"King of Paradise;"* of his infamous estate of marijuana, with other illegal drugs production, and debauched lifestyle among the islanders. Conclusively, the end of the Play presents Burns' allusive "ploughman" as *Papa Bois;* who it would seem, is the real *"King of Paradise,"* whose continuous reign is supported by the island's revolutionaries – the local community. The supernatural denouement is that the omniscient storyteller, at the beginning of the play, believed to be Moses, a Tour Guide of *Paradise Nature Reserve,* was in fact, the legendary and illusive *Papa Bois* in disguise! Subsequently, the expectation is that this story will be perpetuated in repeated transmissions of the folktale, that *Papa Bois*, *"Guardian of the Forest,"* had avenged Dennis, for his wilful and wanton destruction of the land and its inhabitants.

Roselle Thompson
London, 2022

INTRODUCTION

NOTES TO THE INTRODUCTION

1. **Papa Bois -** In Caribbean Folktales, **Papa Bois,** also called **Maitre Bois**, is perhaps the most widely known of Caribbean folklore characters. He is known by many names including "**Maître Bois**" (master of the woods) and "**Daddy Bouchon**" (hairy man).
2. The word **Mama D'Leau**, is derived from the French Maman de l'eau or "Mother of the water/river" (also written as Mama Glo), is the protector and healer of all river animals.
3. **Maroon** – A term derived from Spanish *Cimarron,* meaning 'wild or unruly', refers to slaves in various parts of the Caribbean who, during slavery, ran away from slave plantations to create their own groups and communities as a strategy of resistance. Historically, these independent groups lived on the periphery of slave societies and were particularly prevalent in Brazil, Suriname, and Jamaica. In the context of this play, it refers to the practice of maroon society, e.g., the communal activity in challenging situations. This is shown by their autonomy, group strength, independence, self-determination, and self-reliance. In the Eastern Caribbean, a large gang of workmen would voluntarily join forces to either plough a person's gardens during the planting season or assist in the moving and re-building of a house.
4. **Caribs, Arawaks & Tainos** – the first peoples of the Caribbean. They were Amerindians tribes from as early as 8000BC.
5. *Creole* (noun); a word which originated during the colonial era, is a person of mixed Europeans, (e.g., British, French, Spanish, Dutch) Amerindians and Africans. Used as an adjective, the term is used to refer to the process of creolisation.

INTRODUCTION

6. ***Mulatto*** or ***mulato*** in Spanish: A term used to refer to the offspring of a Negro and white European. In the Caribbean this would have been children of slaves and slave masters.
7. Ehusani, G. O. (1991). *'An Afro-Christian vision (Ozovehe): Towards a more humanized world.'* Lanham, MD: University Press of America.
8. **Crick-crack storytelling** - These African folktale traditions are well-known and practised within the Caribbean territories. Whilst some may vary in renditions, they are all variants from a common origin. One major characteristic in the storytelling is that it embodies performance. The 'Crick Crack' storytelling is a group performance in which the 'audience' participates in a close connection between the performer or storyteller and the audience. It presents an African format of a leader or storyteller and a chorus which is the audience, participating in a whole storytelling session.
9. In other parts of the Caribbean e.g., St. Lucia, the storytelling is performed in French Creole or Patois and the Leader or Conteur, does a similar announcement that the story is about to be told, by calling out "Crick!" ("Kwik" in patois), to which the audience responds by shouting "Crack!"" or "Kwak!" Once the utterance "crick-crack" is completed, the Leader/Conteur continues by testing the audience with riddles, to which they would shout out the answers, in a session of exchanges. After this the story is told. The audience then becomes a chorus that is not only listening but also commenting. Often the riddles and exchanges are about their environment or what is known to them.
10. Thomas J. J. (1869:1969): ***Theory and Practice of Creole Grammar,*** New Beacon Books, London & Trinidad.
11. Campbell, Horace. (1987) ***Rasta and Resistance***. Trenton, N.J.: Africa World Press.

INTRODUCTION

12. Allsop R. (1996,2003;2010): **Dictionary of Caribbean English Usage;** New York, OUP.
13. **Kwéyòl Dictionary** (2001);compiled by Paul Crosbie, David Frank, Emanuel Leon, Peter Samuel; Ed. David Frank; Ministry of Education, Government of St. Lucia. **ALSO,** A Dictionary OF Jamaican English (2002): F.G. Cassidy (Ed) R.B. LePage (Ed). University of the West Indies. **ALSO,** Stephanie Ovide (1996) Creole-English/English-Creole (Caribbean): Concise Dictionary, Hippocrene Books.
14. Burns, Robert (1785): Poem entitled, **'To a Mouse, on turning her up in her nest with the plough,'** Verse 7; But Mousie, thou art no thy-lane,
    > In proving foresight may be vain:
    > The best laid schemes o' Mice an' Men
    > Gang aft agley,
    > An' lea'e us nought but grief an' pain,
    > For promis'd joy!
15. CARICOM Secretariat. *CARICOM.* **Our Caribbean Community: An Introduction.** Kingston: Ian Randle Publishers, 2005.
16. **The American Dream,** rooted in the American Declaration of Independence, is a national ethos of the United States; a belief in a set of ideals (democracy, rights, liberty, opportunity, and equality), in which equality of opportunity is available to any American, allowing the highest aspirations and goals to be achieved through hard work. According to the Dream, this includes the opportunity for one's children to grow up and receive a good education and career without artificial barriers.
17. **W. Shakespeare:** Macbeth (1607:2005): Act 5 Sc.3 Pg 95 Wordsworth Classics

PAPA BOIS:
KING OF PARADISE

CHARACTERS

Moses, *Paradise Nature Reserve* Tour Guide/*Papa Bois*
Patrick & Ella, *Canadian Eco-tourists in the Caribbean*
Hawkers – *local street sellers*
Postman 1 – *in the Caribbean*
Postman 2 – *in the USA*
George & Pamela Palmer – *Caribbean immigrants to America*
Dennis Palmer – *George & Pamela's American-born son*
Ashley & Viola Palmer – Local *Community leaders – George Palmer's brother and sister-in-law*
Matteo & Valeria – *Italian immigrants to America*
Gino – *Matteo & Valeria's American-born son*
Stacey – *Dennis Palmer's girlfriend*
Rev. Truman – *Church Pastor and Community Elder*
Congregation – *Ivy, Nelly, Lydia, Gloria, Anne, Seema, Verna*
Mr. Bright – *a Politician*
Itran ⎱
Egbert   *Local community members*
Isaac ⎰
Zack ⎱
Ed   *Dennis' local, American Gangsters*
Stan ⎰
Filippo ⎱ *Drug Lords*
Juan   ⎰
Big T – *bodyguard to Drug Lords*
Azacca – Rastafarian Representative
Reggie ⎱
Mikey
Alan   *Barber shop Customers & local rebels*
Leslie
Noah   ⎰
Locations: USA & A Caribbean island

PROLOGUE

PROLOGUE

STAGE DIRECTION: The stage is floodlit in soft red, blue and yellow colours, with Caribbean music playing in the background.

Our Caribbean Folktales exist to make people wise;
This is a story of Papa Bois, and the King of Paradise.
Maybe one of the most widely known of our folklore,
But our Papa Bois is known by many names; for sure.
"Maître Bois" (Father of the woods) in French Creole,
Or "Daddy Bouchon" (hairy man), so we were all told.
This old man who lives deep into the country's forest,
Protector of animals, Custodian of trees, he is the best.
You'll know him because he gets animals out of snares,
We know he treats them when sick; but you he'll scare.

Look out, as Papa Bois appears in many different forms:
He is as hairy as an animal, dressed in clothes all worn.
In a pair of ragged trousers, or with a horn in his belt,
Can turn himself into a deer and his anger may be felt.
See his cloven hoofs, leaves growing even in his beard,
May lead bad hunters into the forest to feel his dread.
He may vanish to warn, or force erring men to comply,
And is known to sound a horn, so those at risk can fly.
Be advised he doesn't tolerate killing for killing's sake,
Or for man's wanton greed, destruction will be his fate.

In our folktales there's always some advice to the listener:
Should you meet Papa Bois, know you're not his prisoner.
"Bon jour, Vieux Papa, Bon Matin, Maître," you must greet,
If he stops near you, stay cool, and don't look at his feet!
He's usually very kind, can be dangerous when he's about,

PROLOGUE

He'll cast a spell on a bad man: so you'd better watch out!
Dennis our anti-hero, paid no attention; did not pay heed,
Build cocaine enterprise, sold products from ganga seed.
His story's a tragedy because our traditions he despised,
So this tale is about how his ignorance led to his demise.

ACT 1 SCENE 1 – *WELCOME TO PARADISE!*

On a Caribbean island. In a cocktail bar, at Paradise Nature Reserve, sitting around a table with tall glasses of icy-cold drinks, are tourists Ella and Patrick, who are joined by Moses, whom they believe is their elderly local Tour Guide. Fanning themselves from the heat as they relax, Moses' storytelling introduces them to the background to the King of Paradise story, and the creation of Paradise Nature Reserve.

MOSES	*(approaches guests at a table)* Welcome to *Paradise Nature Reserve*, you must be Ella and Patrick.
PATRICK	*(Standing and shaking hands)* And you must be Moses, our Tour Guide.
MOSES	*(to Ella)* You could say that, and you're both in for a real treat.
ELLA	*(raises her glass)* Nowadays, we're into Eco-tourism, can't wait to dive in; had enough of the beaches and sand tourism over the years.
MOSES	Well, *Paradise Nature Reserve* is one place you won't regret touring. Now in its 10th year celebration, it marks the historic, cultural and heritage site, a place that is unique in value, unequalled by all of nature worldwide.
PATRICK	Impressive! I must say, of all the Eco-tourism Brochures we were bombarded with, we think *Paradise Nature Reserve* stands out as the best to explore, *(rubs his hands animatedly)*, so here we are!
MOSES	OK good. Now, you probably heard that this place was once called *Paradise Island*, owned by a young, notorious, American

1:1   PAPA BOIS: KING OF PARADISE

                            entrepreneur, Dennis Palmer; dubbed *"King of Paradise!"* *(laughs out loudly)* But this so-called *king* is dead! So, I say, long live the real king, *Papa Bois*, and his *Paradise Nature Reserve!*

PATRICK   *(eyeing Ella)* Well Sir, we did do some background reading about this place and there really seems to be something oddly fascinating about it.

MOSES   *(animated)* Ah! But the story didn't begin there. Not at all! This Papa, *(pointing to himself)*, Moi, is the only one who could enlighten you about the real story of *Paradise Island*, and what a story it is! Tomorrow, will be your Tour on the Reserve, but If you have the time right now, just sit back and I'll tell you the story; like no one else can! *(rubs his hands in glee)*

ELLA   *(sounding upbeat)* Well, time is certainly one thing we have a lot of right now, so please sit down Moses, tell us about this *King of Paradise!*

MOSES   *(joins them at the table)* Now, I remember this story as if it was yesterday, because there was a Maroon. *(pausing to think)* Let's see now, it was Isaac's Maroon. Everyone, including me, was waiting to have this Maroon for a while; the selected trees were marked for cutting *J'ouvert,* on that day.

PATRICK   Wait, wait; Jou... what?

MOSES   Well, we the old folks say it in French Creole, *J'ouvert,* means *fore day morning,* as we say

	in local parlance, but for you, I would just say, *day break*.
ELLA	*(excited, sips her drink)* And hey, not so fast – you also said someone had a Maroon? What's that?
MOSES	Yes, it was a fella called Isaac's maroon. And a maroon is our tradition of moving a house, by dismantling it from one place, (in the morning), and then re-building it back together again, (in the evening), before the day is over.
PATRICK	*(surprised)* You mean, breaking down and building back a house – and doing all this in one day?
MOSES	Yes, we do it all the time. With the *Father of the Forest's* help, all must be done before it gets dark. But it's only possible if everyone come together and join in taking down the house in whole sections, and help to put those pieces back together again quickly. *(sips his drink)* There's no hotel or bed-and-breakfast motel to check into, so the occupants must have somewhere to sleep in, that same night!
ELLA	*(excitedly)* Wow! I must say, it sounds like good economic sense!
MOSES	Yes, but the real economy is in cutting down the right amount of trees you need, and not taking one single tree more. That's our traditional way of living in harmony with nature and the forest!

1:1   PAPA BOIS: KING OF PARADISE

PATRICK	Really? Then, I have to say that's one of the earliest conservation measures, I've ever heard of!
MOSES	Well, it comes from an old slave tradition. You see, runaway slaves used to do this, to create their own community; so following the rules of the forest, and with help from the ancestors, everyone joined together to instantly help that runaway remake his life, and to become self-sufficient. *(Vendors walking around, selling their goods, interrupt the conversation)*
VENDOR 1	*(plying their trade to Patrick)* Mister, you want to buy some fruit?
MOSES	*(irritated, gestures with hands)* No, they don't, Go!
VENDOR 1	*(startled, moves away quickly)* Sorry, Papa! **[Exits]**
MOSES	*(angrily grunts, points to the door)* Go!
VENDOR 2	*(sneaks up to Ella)* Look, Madam, it's the cheapest you will find out here.
ELLA	*(shakes her head)* Looks nice, but not today, thank you!
MOSES	*(stands, eyes flashing, holds a horn)*
VENDOR 2	*(looks surprised)* Oh, it's you, Papa!
MOSES	*(points to the entrance door)* You too, don't even bother coming here. Just go. Now!
VENDOR 2	*(hurrying, bows)* I'm going. Bon Matin, Maître. **[Exits]**
MOSES	*(sitting, clears his throat)* One thing I will tell you is this; the end of *Paradise Island* became the beginning, or the making of

1:1 PAPA BOIS: KING OF PARADISE

Paradise Nature Reserve, which you'll see tomorrow.

PATRICK *(puzzled, eyes Ella)* Hold on! Bartender, fill up our glasses again. *(glances at Moses)* Then we'll be all ears. Don't want to miss a thing.

ELLA You know, Moses, what I'm most fascinated by, is the miraculous ways that they claim unique species of animals and birds have found themselves in *Paradise Nature Reserve*, with absolutely no one's assistance, intervention, or maintenance!

PATRICK *(sitting down)* And what about crops growing there that haven't been planted by anyone, and they say, don't exist anywhere in the world, except in *Paradise Nature Reserve*. How can this be?

MOSES *(smiles coyly, nods)* Well, let's just say they had natural assistance. *(smiling, sips his drink)* And what you say *is* true. In fact, I'd say only the old folks and *Papa Bois*, might have the real answers to your questions.

ELLA So, why the old folks? And again, sorry, but what exactly d'you mean?

MOSES Well, the answers are more to do with the legendary *Papa Bois, Guardian of the Forest*, who they all say is the real *King of Paradise*. When Dennis Palmer, the American boy, came here and cut down an entire estate of good, wholesome, natural land, he planted and manufactured marijuana and other drugs products instead. He traded in cocaine and guns from north and south America, and

1:1   PAPA BOIS: KING OF PARADISE

	everyone knew that *Papa Bois* was not going to let him succeed. You see, the land is the soul and heart-beat of a country, and the birth-right of its people, especially the young.
ELLA	*(nodding in agreement)* I see, wasn't Dennis born in America, but his parents were Caribbean people, right from this very place, I believe?
MOSES	Yes, and welcomed, he sure was. But he shouldn't have disrespected the land as he did. What he did was like cursing it, or poisoning the very lungs that breathed and give life to the folks. *(laugh nervously)* And disrespecting us too. We weren't going to stand for that! That is why old people say, *Papa Bois*, got rid of him with a revolutionary fire on the Estate!
ELLA	Wow! That's one way of putting it. I heard that this *Papa Bois* is responsible for the present globally famous *Paradise Nature Reserve,* which he's supposed to look after, even to this day! Is that true?
MOSES	Yes, that *is* true. We, the old folks, always say, *'as it was in the beginning, so shall it be in the end'* – meaning with *Papa Bois* being there from the beginning of time, the land, good people, and future thriving generations, will continue to live peacefully, to the end of time!
PATRICK	*(passing cocktail glasses around)* I see. So are you saying this *Papa Bois* legend is somehow still trending?

1:1   PAPA BOIS: KING OF PARADISE

MOSES *(surprised)* Trending? Look, as clearly as you see me sitting here before you, *Papa Bois* and his story, is alive and well; right here and now, and throughout this land!

PATRICK *(half-joking)* So what are we dealing with, Moses? *(Jokingly)* Sounds just like you have some type of *Big Foot* or *Yeti*, in your Garden-of-Eden or Paradise Nature Reserve?

ELLA *(half-laughing, shrugs)* Yes, y'know, like in the Bible; only in this one there's no Adam and Eve! *(laughs loudly)*

MOSES *(with a serious glare)* Let's just say before it all began, I was instrumental in helping to preserve the land; before the creation of *Paradise Nature Reserve*. So, from first-hand experience, I can tell you that the kind of Paradise you'll see now, is nothing like it used to be, when the so-called American *King of Paradise* was its owner. *(voice lowers to a whisper)* You see, he was **never** really *the King*.

ELLA & MOSES *(looking puzzled, stared at each other)*

MOSES It all started like this……

[Curtains]

ACT 1 SCENE 2 – *THE BEST LAID SCHEMES*

A sunny day in a Caribbean island. On a veranda in Viola Palmer's house. A radio is playing in the background. A Postman arrives with a letter for her from Pamela, her migrant sister-in-law and husband George, who's settled in the USA.

POSTMAN	*(humming)* Morning Miss V, ah got a registered letter for you today.
VIOLA	Eh heh?
POSTMAN	Yes ma'am, all the way from the US of A!
VIOLA	Ah, it can only be from one person, and that's my sister-in-law Pamela. Thank you, mister postman!
POSTMAN	*(hands the letter)* Don't thank me yet. I hope it brings good news to thank me about another day. Only then, I'll say I'm the bearer of good news, Miss V. *(laughs as he leaves).*
VIOLA	*(opening the letter, yells)* Ashley! Ashley! Come noh!
ASHLEY	*(rushing)* Okay, Okay, where's the fire! Girl you go bring up meh blood pressure. What you hurrying me so for?
VIOLA	*(animatedly)* Come, ah get letter from America – Come leh we read it, man.
ASHLEY	*(sitting next to her)* Yes, so what she saying now?
VIOLA	*(opens the letter and reads)* "My Dearest Sister V, Greetings, I the name of our Lord Jesus. I hope this letter finds you and Ashley in good health, as it leaves us.

1:2   PAPA BOIS: KING OF PARADISE

George, Dennis, and me are all well, thank God.
As you know, things over here with jobs have been going well, and I know we are lucky to be in steady, employment, so we can save and carry out our long-term goals for coming back home; y'know, like I said before, to gain our 'American Dream' in the Caribbean! (laugh). So right now, we really want to beat the iron while it's still hot."

ASHLEY OK, so when they coming back?
VIOLA Hold on noh man, there's more; leh me continue.

"After braving the cold all these years in New York, we think it's high time to return home. As y'know, we didn't expect to stay here that long, but at least we can now buy land to build a house on, and get an income from it; then we will be able to coast through our twilight years in comfort.
What I'm trying to say is, I think our search for a 10-acre plot of land in the right spot, might finally be over. George's been negotiating with a Developer over there; you might even know him. His name is Alvin Renwick, with an office somewhere in town. George's been talking to him about buying this 10-acre piece of land, but of course, as you'd expect, there is competition. It seems we're not the only one going after it."

ASHLEY *(Butts in)* I've heard about this Renwick fella. In fact, they're Big Land Developers and Home Buying Agents, at the end of Market

1:2 PAPA BOIS: KING OF PARADISE

Hill Street, in town. They're the biggest on the island; especially for retiring Caribbean people from abroad.

VIOLA But hold on, I'm not finished, there's more....

"That's why we want you and Ashley to go and see this fella called Renwick really quick, explore the land for us and report back as soon as you can. He says it has plenty cocoa and nutmeg, with enough space to propagate all kinds of produce to live off the land. As you know, we're not shy to work on the land, and we hope Dennis will grow to like the idea of moving from America to the Caribbean for good, eventually. It's been difficult convincing him of holidaying in the Caribbean, let alone, settling there for good! But more on that later, let's tackle Renwick as an urgent first step, then leave the rest to God. Renwick's telephone number is 010......."

ASHLEY *(excitedly)* Well, it's good news, and as they say, let's make hay while the sun shines. So give me his phone number; ah calling him right now. *(Dials the number)*

VOICE *(voice on the end of the telephone line)* 'Hello, Affordable Caribbean! .... Yes, this is Renwick speaking. Uh huh...I see. Yes, Mr. Palmer, I do remember talking to your relatives from the States. They did ask me to look out for your call. Uh huh.. Yes... I believe the other interested party has an appointment for next Friday. Uh huh.... How soon can you come to see me then? Uh huh.. OK, then, can you come to my office tomorrow morning at 11am sharp?'

ASHLEY 'Wow! Ah couldn't expect any better. Yes Sir! Tomorrow's good, the time's good too. Uh huh…OK… So, we'll see tomorrow then. Thanks eh, Bye!'

VIOLA *(pats him on the back)* Ashley Palmer, that's what you call beating the iron while it's hot. Now we ready for him, tomorrow!

ASHLEY Well, isn't that what they say, *Do it Now!* *(nudges her)* Y'hear that? *(winks at her)*, *Do it now*!

VIOLA *(looking coyly at him)* Sure Babes, we making hay while the sun shine too!

ASHLEY *(affectionately puts his her around her shoulder)* Girl, you know what, ah can't wait for those two to come back home; it would be just like in the old days, man.

VIOLA Yes, I know. This just proves what they say, eh; 'There's no place like home.' You roam all around the world, but in the end, *home* is really where the heart is, eh.

ASHLEY It's true, look how all man, Jack, and their brother, leave this country, running away with great speed, like a ball. And what happen in the long run? They rebound and bounce right back here – back to where? *Home!*

VIOLA It's true, whether they run to America, Canada, England or anywhere around this Caribbean region, deep down inside of every one of them, *home* will always be calling them back.

ASHLEY   Yes, it would be great to see my big brother George again. And when they come back here, people like you and me girl, are right here, to welcome them.

VIOLA   Bwoy, leh me say Amen to that!

[Curtains]

ACT 1 SCENE 3 – *A SENSE OF BELONGING*

It's Christmas in New York, and Pamela, George, and Dennis, Palmer are around their Christmas dinner table, with invited guests - their American neighbours, who are Matteo, Valeria, and their son Gin, in their seasonally decorated Dining Room, soft Christmas carols are playing in the background.

GEORGE	*(passing a bowl)* Well, it's Christmas in New York again! A non-stop tradition, year in, year out. Matteo you have to try this, Pam's added some extra special Caribbean delights this year. If all goes to plan, then this may be our last Christmas meal together, before we set sail, back home to the Caribbean, for good.
MATTEO	*(putting food from the bowl onto his plate)* Thanks. We're sure going to miss you guys. We've been neighbours for what seems like forever! And I really can't imagine you-all no longer being here, as our neighbours after all these years.
VALERIA	Yes, we've been neighbours for a decade now. You could say, we're like family now. I really can't believe you-all are really leaving.
PAMELA	*(trying to sound upbeat)* Hey, c'm on, it doesn't have to end here. In fact, you'll now have the Caribbean as a place to come and visit us in, and I insist it's got to be every year, right George?
GEORGE	Yes, just think of it as gaining another home, another country, more family to broaden your horizon, with everlasting sun, sea, and

1:3   PAPA BOIS: KING OF PARADISE

	land. So you could say it's a win-win situation, really.
MATTEO	And what does young Dennis have to say about that?
PAMELA	*(eyeing her son)* Well Dennis, I think this question is for you to answer.
DENNIS	*(putting his glass down)* Dunno the answer Uncle Matt. *(shrugs)* But, whatever!
PAMELA	*(sternly)* No, Honey, they want to hear what you really have to say on the subject; just say what you feel. They're like family, so you can talk.
DENNIS	*(finishing his second glass of wine)* Seriously? You guys really want to know what I think *(nervous laughs)* about going to live in a place that I've never set foot in and don't know about?
GEORGE	*(snaps at him)* Yes, and why not? As I've said too many times before, I too, had to uproot, leave family and everything behind back home in the Caribbean, to come to live here in America. It was a place I didn't know anything about, apart from the fact that I would get a job, and the belief that if I worked hard enough, I would earn enough to help the family back home.
PAMELA	Yes, the plan was to eventually make something of ourselves, buy a piece of land back home and build a house on it, to settle down in our old age.
MATTEO	Well, that was my plan too, I had to do the exact same! I too left Italy as a young man, about you and Gino's age. Everyone had

	their sights set high, to make something of themselves abroad, feed families back home, whether it was going to America, England, or Canada. At only 20 years, we were brave young men and women.
VALERIA	Yes, we were brave to leave our families in Italy and come to America, to meet with whatever fate had in store for us. *(sighs loudly)* We were scared sometimes, but knew we *had to* have a go of trying to succeed and at the same time, save up and send for members of our family to join us here! We did it because we knew we *had to*!
GEORGE	You can say that again! All we knew was, you had to work to send money back home to help the family and manage ourselves out here; whatever the weather or season. Your mom came to work as a Nurse, and I got work in a car factory. And guess what, we made it! Look at us today, at least we have something to show for it, **our own** *American dream!*
VALERIA	Yes, now that Matteo and I managed to buy our own home here, and you guys bought yours back in the Caribbean. You could say, our plans did work for both of us. *(glancing over at her son)* Gino, you OK. You seem a little quiet over there.
GINO	*(nodding)* Hmm! Just enjoying all this delicious Caribbean Christmas food!
GEORGE	*(chuckles)* Well, 'tis the season to be merry. Although Christmas here is not quite like it is

	back home. *(holds his hands up)* Hey, I'm not complaining, we always make the most of it. *(to his son)* Steady, there Dennis, I notice you're drinking wine and mixing it up with *Puncha Crema;* you know that simple-looking drink is strong stuff, right!
DENNIS	*(laughing loudly)* Uh huh! It does have a big kick to it. *(coughs)* Don't worry you-all. I think I can handle it. *(holds out his glass, pretending to be drunk)* Just pass me some more!
PAMELA	*(half-serious)* It's true Dennis, not so fast. Slow down and pace yourself. You already had more than 3 glasses of wine. And you still have more gorgeous food to eat, right?
GINO	As for me, I always love feasting on aunty Pam's Caribbean food. Aunty, I tell you it's the best! Sorry mum, no offence!
VALERIA	Oh Gino! *(laughing)* Today, mama can take 2nd place.
GINO	And today more so, because as you say, it might be my last Christmas Caribbean dinner before you-all leave us here for good.
PAMELA	Thanks for the compliments, Gino. Here, Hon, have some more of this one.
GINO	So Aunty Pam, you're going back to the Caribbean, but it's not quite *going back* for Dennis, he's never been there! I can imagine doing something like that would be tough for me. Because I've never been anywhere else; even for College - just stayed here. Good old New York, the *Big Apple*, where everyone longs to be; 'the City that never sleeps.'

1:3   PAPA BOIS: KING OF PARADISE

DENNIS   *(half-laughing, half-serious)* Well, I imagine they don't even have a city that's even awake in the Caribbean! Not quite in the 20th century yet, I gather, from you-all stories about your back home! The place sounds backward to me, I don't know!

GEORGE   *(Sternly)* Backward? Nonsense! You could've experienced what's currently happening, if only you'd agreed to go there with us for holidays at least once, and not be so pig-headed, and arrogant; the dozens of times we begged you to.

DENNIS   *(embarrassed)* Yeah dad. I know, I know. Don't rub it in.

GEORGE   Remember, instead of coming with us, you chose to stay in America, going here there and everywhere. If it wasn't summer camps, or boating on lakes, it was Chicago, Atlanta, Vegas; just going around and around in America! Christ! You behave as if America's the only place on earth!

DENNIS   *(raising his voice)* Dad, I just know the Caribbean isn't ready for me yet. I think they haven't caught up with 20th century pace of life. And as for technology, to me, that place is bereft of real life and technological advancement. Now that I've finished college, I'm ready to spread my wings, so we'll just have to wait and see.

PAMELA   *(whispering)* OK, OK, you two, that's enough at the dinner table. It's Christmas!

1:3 PAPA BOIS: KING OF PARADISE

MATTEO *(looking for support)* George, my friend, it's a shame, that young people these days want everything handed to them on a plate.

GEORGE Exactly!

MATTEO I blame the 20th century for taking away their tenacity and pride in working hard, instead of getting everything done by pressing buttons on computers; and to me, they rarely seem to be doing a hard day's work!

GEORGE *(nodding)* I agree with you, Matt. A long time ago, there were days my friend, when we didn't dare hide behind excuses, but just did what we had to, to survive.

VALERIA *(getting up)* Here Pam, let me help you take these plates to the kitchen. *[Exits]*

PAMELA *(clearing the table)* I won't say no, Val. I'm going to bring in the desert next. *[Exits]*

GEORGE So Gino, your father tells me you have an upcoming interview at the famous Smithsonian Marketing Institute.

GINO Yes, I've already had 2 other job interviews but with no luck, so with these past experiences under my belt, I'm hoping to get this one.

GEORGE What's it for?

GINO It's for a Publicity and Marketing Consultant, answerable to the Regional Manager. But I might have a similar dilemma as Dennis, like moving out of New York to Boston. That is, if I get it. Their reputation and their pay is good. So wish me luck!

1:3 PAPA BOIS: KING OF PARADISE

GEORGE	Good luck! But you know Gino, it really would be their loss, if they don't hire you. *(pats Gino on the back)* You're a good kid.
GINO	Uncle George, you're so good for my ego right now, thanks.
GEORGE	Now, take young Dennis here, his superior skills and qualifications in animal husbandry, soil taxonomy and soil formation process, makes him a unique candidate to monopolise growth and development of land, especially in the Caribbean; he could make millions of dollars. But then, he doesn't believe or have that vision, so it's all up to him to decide his fate.
DENNIS	You said it, dad. It's not my vision. You know my goal's the music industry, where I have a vision and already making a future. There's success there for me, you'll see.
GEORGE	*(shakes head, holds up his hands)* OK, OK, Son! I give in, for now!
PAMELA	*(Returns animatedly with the desert)* Here it comes guys! Now you-all know the famous Caribbean black cake but today, I've added something extra - sweet potato pone with double cream, custard or ice cream, or everything together! Pass these around.
VALERIA	*(sitting down)* Wow Pam! Don't mind if I do! Mmm! *(Desert is eaten to grunts and sounds of pleasurable approval)*
GINO	Mmm, it's so good!
DENNIS	You've done it again, mum. Delicious!

1:3   PAPA BOIS: KING OF PARADISE

MATTEO	Compliments to our lovely cook, Pam, I'm having 2nds and 3rds! And licking the pot!
VALERIA	Mmm! I'm having the best time ever, you-all.
GEORGE	*(standing, clinks wine glass)* Attention everybody! A toast! Here's to good friends, good times with family, and having lots more fun with you-all in the Caribbean, in the future. *(raises his glass)* Merry Christmas! and a Happy New Year!
MATTEO	*(Stands)* Hear! Hear! *Buon Natale* to our best friends and family.
VALERIA	*(Stands)* And *Buon Anno,* with lots of my love too!
GINO	*(Stands)* I wish you the same! *Felice anno nuovo!*
DENNIS	*(Stands)* To my dearest Italian-American family, as you say, *Altrettanto!* To our future and the good times to come.

The volume of the Christmas background music increases

[Curtains]

Glossary
Buon Natale – Merry Christmas
Buon Anno – Happy New Year
Felice anno nuovo – Happy New Year
Altrettanto! – and the same to you!

ACT 1 SCENE 4 – *A MUSICAL ACCOLADE*

At an annual Music Award ceremony event. Dennis is a nominee for The Best Newcomer of the Year in the Hip Hop music category. He is attending the ceremony with his parents, friends, and media influencers, as guests at his table.

GEORGE (*Sitting around a table, turns to Dennis*) Well son, this is a big night for you, I'm glad to be here, sharing this special night with you.

DENNIS Thanks dad, I'm glad too!

PAMELA (*turning to her son, lowers her voice*) Yes, and remember hon, it's not always about winning, just being part of it is also good too. (*sighing*) I mean, if I'm this nervous and I'm not even taking part, I can't imagine how you're feeling now.

DENNIS (*patting his mum on her arm*) Yes, mum, I'm nervous like hell too, but don't worry. (*winks at his mum*) And I guess, so is every single nominee in this room too!

PAMELA (*whispering*) I mean, they think you're good enough to be nominated, so you should win, but whatever happens, remember we love you lots, and you'll always be our little star!

DENNIS (*nervously rubbing his hands*) Thanks dad, mum, appreciate you-all being here. Let's just see what the night brings, eh.
(*the Masters of Ceremony, take the stage to announce the next category of winners*)

MC 1 This year has really been a bumper year for the music industry, what with the amount of outstanding artists out there, keeping our

1:4	PAPA BOIS: KING OF PARADISE

	nation, and the world, entertained in more ways than one; creating theirs and our history, and the sweet music just keep rolling on and on! *(loud applause)*
MC 2	Yes, we have been spoilt for choice as you can see so far. But now we must keep it moving, by going to the next category of nominees, which is, the *Best Newcomer of the Year* in the *Hip Hop Category*. And the nominees are Peter James, Sam Walker, Louis Abraham, and Dennis Palmer. *(loud applause)*
MC1	*(opening an envelope)* Yes, in these envelopes, are the nation's choice for the *Best Newcomer of the Year in the Hip Hop Category*. So, in 3rd place is... Sam Walker! *(loud applause)* In the 2nd place, is... Peter James! *(loud applause)*
MC 2	And ladies and gentlemen, in this Winner's envelope is your choice for *The Best Newcomer of the Year* in the *Hip Hop* Category. Drum roll please. *(opens the envelope)* I can now tell you.. that in 1st place... the winner is... Dennis Palmer! *(thunderous applause as Dennis stands and makes his way to the podium on stage)*
MC1	Wow! Congratulations goes to you Dennis. I have pleasure in presenting you with this well-deserved award. Long may you reign, delighting hip-hop fans and keeping the music alive. *(hands him an accolade and shakes his hand).* Well done! *(thunderous applause)*

1:4   PAPA BOIS: KING OF PARADISE

DENNIS *(general silence, as he takes the microphone)* Wow! Wow! First of all, I wanna thank everyone who nominated and believe in me! This really means a lot to me, and really not just me, there's a whole bunch of people involved in making all of this possible. I wanna thank my parents, who're sitting over there, for always supporting me. *(applause)* *(pointing)* My producer, over there, John Barnes. *(applause)* Stand, John, *(gestures love, as he touches his heart)*, my band members, *(applause)* who're all sitting over there – *(motions to them, they stand in turn)* Eddy Love, DJ King, and party-man, Jukes! Thanks guys, **we** did it! And thanks to this great organization for recognising all our efforts.
(thunderous applause as Dennis leaves the stage, returns to his seat as the proceedings continue)

MC2 Ladies and gentlemen, we have come to the end of this brilliant evening, satisfied that this industry has shown that it'll stand the test of time, excelling to great heights; confidently knowing that the stars of tonight will be the drivers of great music in our Country, for a long time to come.

MC1 Yes, and may each musician here tonight, whether nominated or not, along with tonight's awardees, continue to lead the way globally, and show the true quality of what we have to offer them, through the language

1:4   PAPA BOIS: KING OF PARADISE

	of music. *(thunderous applause)* So, it's Good night from us, and thank you-all.
MC2	We'll see you-all again at next year's event. *(whistles, applause, standing ovation, as music becomes louder)*
	Outside, at the entrance of the Award Ceremony building
GINO	*(patting Dennis' back, they embrace)* Hey bro, congratulations, you're the man!
GEORGE	*(shakes his hand and they hug)* Well done, Son. Our first and only musician in the family. I'm so proud of you.
PAMELA	*(weeping)* My little boy's now a big star. *(holds her arms out to him)* You make your mama proud. *(embraces him)*
DENNIS	*(hugging her)* Couldn't have done it without having the best mum and dad in the world! And the night's not over yet. We're all going to celebrate at The *Rendezvous Club*, and you must come too.
GEORGE	You sure? *(looks at Pamela)* Maybe I should take your mother home. Been a long day, not sure about holding out late into the night, *(looks at his watch)* or shall I say early morning.
DENNIS	*(jokingly teases)* Hey dad, you're not getting too old to shake those legs, are you!
GEORGE	*(laughs, joking)* In my days, I could out-dance everyone - even you!
DENNIS	*(cheeky banter)* Prove it then, bring mum, take her for a spin on the dance floor; I promise I'll let you take her home straight after that, eh?

1:4   PAPA BOIS: KING OF PARADISE

PAMELA   Oh Honey, I'm dead beat now. Y'know, we'll celebrate with you another time, just the 3 of us, but as for the rest of tonight, it's for you youngsters. I insist, go and have fun, and enjoy yourselves.

DENNIS   OK, mum, if you're absolutely sure you want to go home, I'll hail a cab. *(she nods)* Thanks for being here on my big night mum! *(hugs her and pecks her on the cheek)* Love you, you're the best!

GEORGE   Now you youngsters take it easy, and be safe. Which one of you's going to drive? *(sternly)* Not been drinking, I hope?

DENNIS   Oh Dad, stop fussing, we'll be fine. No one's driving. We're all going to the *Rendezvous* by taxis. Here, take my Award home. *(calls a passing taxi)* Taxi! Here's one now. *(once they're inside, Dennis leans through the window, teases).* OK, Mr. and Mrs Early-nighters, go home, chill, and we'll catch up in the morning. *(whispers to them)* Tonight was perfect, because you were both there!

GEORGE   *(touches his hand)* Your mother and I are the proudest parents tonight, because of you!

DENNIS   *(winks at them)* Thanks. I'll always remember that! *(taxi drives off, Dennis waves till they're out of sight)*

                                                    [Exits}

Several hours later, around 4.00am, outside the Rendezvous Club, everyone is dispersing

DENNIS   *(in high spirits)* Gino, what a night! Thanks again guys, been one of the greatest nights

1:4   PAPA BOIS: KING OF PARADISE

                    of my life. *(Takes his phone off silent mode)*
                    Wow, look at that! My phone's jam-packed
                    with hundreds of missed calls and texts.
GINO   *(looking at his phone)* Hey, me too man, but
                    mine's mostly from dad - and mom!
                    (surprised, reads the 1st text) "Call home
                    urgently!" *(reads 2nd text)* "There's an
                    emergency, call us!" *(reads 3rd text)* "Call
                    now, heading to the County Hospital."
                    Wonder what the heck's going on?
                    (panicking, dials home-phone)
MATTEO   *(relieved, answers phone)* Oh God, at last!
                    Son, I've news; it's not good.
GINO   What! Is it mum? Is she alright?
MATTEO   Yes, your mother's OK.
GINO   So, what's going on, dad?
MATTEO   Where's Dennis, is he with you right now?
GINO   *(looks puzzled)* Yes, Dennis is here. Dad,
                    your voice doesn't sound right. What's
                    wrong?
MATTEO   Son, just put Dennis on the phone now,
                    we've been desperately trying to get hold of
                    you two by phone, all night.
GINO   But dad our phones were on silent and….
MATTEO   *(interrupts sternly & abruptly)* Gino! Just
                    hand the phone to Dennis right now! There's
                    been a terrible road accident!
DENNIS   *(animatedly takes the phone)* Hey Uncle
                    Matt, qué pasa? You heard I won….
MATTEO   *(interrupts)* Listen Dennis, there's some
                    really bad news. I don't know how to tell
                    you, and there's no easy way of breaking it to
                    you. So Imma give it to you straight. There

was a car crash tonight. The Taxi with your parents crashed into a cement truck, the driver died on the spot; he was drunk! Your parents were rushed to the Hospital, but both were pronounced dead on arrival.

DENNIS *(shocked)* What! Dead? Nah, Uncle Matt, don't say that; it can't be.

MATTEO I'm afraid so, son! I wish I could tell you differently. Dennis, I'm so sorry!

DENNIS But, Uncle Matt you said both dead! Surely there must be a mistake? Ah mean, where are they? I don't know.... what to do?

MATTEO They're in Brooklyn County Jewish Hospital. But leh me take you there, eh.

DENNIS *(incoherently, mumbling; the phone away from his ear)* Mum, dad! Dead? Oh God, why?

MATTEO You still there, Dennis? Look, I'll drive you there, the moment you and Gino get here.

DENNIS *(listening, crying loudly)* But Uncle Matt, you said they're both **dead**!

MATTEO I know I said that, and right now, I wish I could tell you differently, Dennis.

DENNIS I mean, Mom and dad, both of them – **dead**? Are you absolutely sure?

MATTEO Yes Dennis, I'm sure. They're gone, and I'm so sorry.
(trancelike, Dennis hands the phone back to Gino then slumps to the ground; mumbling incoherently, trembling uncontrollably)

MATTEO *(consoles Dennis)* I'm so very sorry, Dennis.

1:4 PAPA BOIS: KING OF PARADISE

GINO Dad, it's not Dennis, It's me here. *(bursts into tears)* OK dad! We'll be back as soon as we can.

MATTEO Now listen to me Gino. We all have to hold it together. I also know I don't have to tell you to help Dennis; he'll need us now more than ever. And son, I promise, somehow we'll *all* help Dennis to get through this; one way or the other, OK?

GINO *(crying, sighs)* OK dad, we'll see you soon!

[Curtains]

ACT 2 SCENE 1 - *GRIEF AND PAIN*

Nine months later. At home in New York, Dennis is not coping well with bereavement. Being orphaned at the height of his new-found fame, has forced him into a downward spiral of mental health issues. His home is in disarray, with piles of unopened letters on the floor, and empty alcohol bottles on a table.

There is a knock on the front door. A yawning and unkempt Dennis incautiously opens it.

POSTMAN	*(at the slightly ajar door)* Got a "signed for" international registered letter here for a Dennis Palmer. Wow! didn't think anyone was in. No one's opened this door to me for some months, now!
DENNIS	*(squinting from the light)* Uh huh! I'm Dennis Palmer.
POSTMAN	*(pushing a flipboard to the sleepy receiver)* Sir, here's your letter, sign this please. *(As the front door closes, he immediately throws the letter on a table in the kitchen)*
STACEY	Morning sleepy-head. Who was that at the door?
DENNIS	The postman, with more letters. *(scoffs)* Only this time he brings an international registered one. *(sarcastically)* Yeah right, such a big deal! Could only be from one place, the Caribbean; Uncle Ashley and Aunt Viola.

2:1 PAPA BOIS: KING OF PARADISE

STACEY Well, luckily it's not another bill, and you've lots of them D, so you should open this one, at least. *(trying to sound upbeat)* Won't hurt to hear what the ol' folks have to say to their nephew, eh? Besides, they're your only relatives, who can console you.

DENNIS *(aggressively, voiced raised)* Console me? I'm inconsolable! Whatever they or anyone says, can't bring back mom and dad!

STACEY *(soft tone)* Look D, I know no one can bring them back, but you've got to face up to the world again. Y'know, like take a little step each day, but just keep going. I'm sure your Mom and dad would've wanted you to. *(coaxes as she hands him coffee and pats him on the shoulder)* And as for your relatives, read their letters, hear what they've got to say. Honey, it's been 9 months, try and keep all lines of communication open.

DENNIS *(drinking)* Well, It's probably going to be about their old-time, good-time stories, y'know, Caribbean nostalgia. Things I know nothing about, in that damned place – *(sneers)* their precious Caribbean!

STACEY Stop being so pessimistic! Look, if I've got your permission, I'll read the letter to you, so all you have to do is listen. How about that, eh?

DENNIS *(waves his hand at the letter)* Be my guest, Stace! Knock yourself out! *(sips more coffee, eyeing her, he motions nonchalantly with his hand)* Go on, read, read!

2:1   PAPA BOIS: KING OF PARADISE

STACEY (*surprised*) Okay! But look, stop me at any time you want; ah mean, if it gets too much for you. (*looking at him, clears her throat*) You ready for this? Here goes, (*opens letter*)

To Dennis, our Dearest Nephew,
Greetings in the name of our Lord Jesus.
I hope this letter finds you in good spirits, despite the recent heartaches. At this difficult time, I know that no one can describe or understand the pain you bear, with the passing of your parents - my dear sister-in-law and best friend, and dearest George. There are things in this life we sometimes just can't explain, (and I'm afraid this is one of them); no matter how hard we try. When this happens, we do our best to carry on. That's what I'm appealing to you to do. Dear, dear Dennis, just stay strong, carry on and think about a future for yourself. However, I worry greatly that I've not heard from you, since we were last together at the funeral, and already nine months have flown by, changing all our lives so abruptly, that we muddle through, comforting one another, and doing what your parents would've wanted you to do. Having said that, there's the matter of the 10 acres of land they'd bought here, which needs to be formally executed and transferred to you. This is a small 10-acre estate, producing a lucrative export trade in tropical produce – cocoa, banana, nutmeg, spices, and fruit, as well as

generating local sales within the island, helped by a small workforce of 15 people. There's a grand 6 bedroom house which stands empty, and although your uncle Ashley and I've been overseeing everything for your Late parents, we can't do so indefinitely.

We need you to come over and take on the legal responsibility, and see what your options are in managing such an investment. Your parents had very high hopes of settling here in comfort, in their retirement years, and as such, it's now their legacy to you. So, we need to begin the legal process of transferring the estate to you, as soon as possible; the documents are all ready to be handed over to you. I know it may not be what you want to hear at this time, when you're still hurting inside, but remember, we're both here to guide and support you with whatever you decide to do. Please contact us, as soon as possible, in whatever way you can – by telephoning, telegram, Email, face-timing with Zoom or WhatsApp, writing, or better still, just get on a plane and come! We'll be waiting eagerly to hear from you real soon, and close this letter by sending you our dearest love, lots of hugs and kisses. From your Aunt V. and Uncle Ash.

DENNIS *(shaking his bowed head in contemplation and crying)* Thank you, Stace. *(blows his nose loudly)* Thanks a lot.

2:1   PAPA BOIS: KING OF PARADISE

STACY   *(hugging Dennis)* That's alright love! It ain't that bad, is it? What d'you plan to do, eh?

DENNIS I've no idea, but I'll probably think about what they've said about this Caribbean Estate.

STACEY *(smiling)* Very good! See, already, that's a step in the right direction.

DENNIS *(deep in thought)* I'm just taking one day at a time, Stace; just one day at a time.

STACEY Yes, and that's all we need to do right now; just small steps to a complete recovery. *(kisses his cheek, she holds his hands)* A famous man, facing adversity once said, *"We shall overcome!"* And you my dearest D., you too will overcome. I'll do whatever it takes to help and support you.

DENNIS *(Sighs deeply, loudly)* And when we do Stace, remember, there'll be no going backwards or sideways, just going forward, *(pause then sounding upbeat)*, to overcome!

STACEY *(upbeat)* OK! Now, you're beginning to sound like the old Dennis I used to know! *(giggles)*

                                    [Curtains]

ACT 2 SCENE 2 – *'THEM-AND-US'*

Dennis is inside his inherited 6 bedroomed house in the Caribbean. He is in conversation with his uncle, aunt, and girlfriend, after surveying his entire estate. They sit around a dining table, with drinks and snacks.

ASHLEY	So Dennis, now you've seen everything, tell us what you think, noh.
DENNIS	Well Uncle Ash, I have to say in all honesty, it's really *not* what I'd imagined.
VIOLA	How you mean? It's bad?
DENNIS	Not at all Uncle, on the contrary! I actually expected the place to be in a worse state; meaning the whole island. The fact is, the picture of the Caribbean in my head was far worse than this reality. Sorry, but it's my bad.
ASHLEY	No you're not bad, son.
DENNIS	Uncle I mean, it's my ignorance.
ASHLEY	Well, your parents would never have made a wrong move, God rest their souls.
VIOLA	I say Amen to that!
ASHLEY	And you young lady - Stacey, isn't it! What's *your* verdict so far? Because you say you've never been out of America, how you liking this place?
STACEY	From what I've seen so far, where we've been, and experiences we've had, I would say it's very idyllic; in fact, more like a little paradise.

2:2   PAPA BOIS: KING OF PARADISE

DENNIS (*animatedly*) That's it! I'll call this place *Paradise*, how does that sound?

VIOLA Well yes, *Paradise* is a real good name. (*winks at Dennis*) In truth, your parents would've been proud to know they left you with '*a paradise*!'

ASHLEY Look Dennis, you've got everything you can want here, and more. All I can say is, you're a very lucky young man. And if you play your cards right, you'll be a very wealthy man too.

DENNIS Y'know, Uncle Ash, I remember dad telling me once that I could use my qualification in soil taxonomy and soil formation process, right here. At the time, I laughed at his idea, which I now really regret doing. In fact, I've only just realised that his vision was pretty advanced.

STACEY (*patting his shoulders*) Honey, no regrets, eh; better late than never. Do something good in memory of that, and of them.

DENNIS (*contemplating*) Yeah, that gives me food for thought. In fact, lots of ideas are knocking about in my head right now. It'll mean making some drastic changes that probably won't be popular though, but looks like there's a niche market here, and I intend to exploit it.

ASHLEY Well, labourers are cheap here, with the high unemployment rate, so building a workforce can be fast and easy. But remember, this is a village area and some of the old folks have all kinds of superstitious beliefs, especially when you're a land-owner.

2:2   PAPA BOIS: KING OF PARADISE

DENNIS What d'you mean?
ASHLEY Well, the one thing those who own land seem to live by is an old, old code; based on the legendary *Papa Bois*. Folktale claims he is *Protector of the land*, and tolerates no wanton destruction of the land or killing for killing sake.
STACEY *(laughing)* Y'mean y'all people here believe in folktales, and use them to manage their own possessions?
ASHLEY *(nods agreement)* Look, it's not that simple although it sounds that way! Then there's the contentions between our own people living here and those who lived abroad and come back here to re-settle. Many here see returning nationals as "foreigners." In fact, you almost have to prove yourself to gain their trust; so they'll be watching your every move, Dennis.
VIOLA Yes, the general thinking is that all Caribbean people who come back home to live among us, are jokingly called, *"the mad people!"*
DENNIS Mad? How so?
ASHLEY Firstly, when they come back here they rush around quick-quick in the hot sun; rushing everywhere, demanding things; as if they think they're still in the cold countries abroad. Not realising the pace here is slower for logical reasons. *(laughs)* Anyhow, it's something they realise sooner or later, then eventually slow down to fit in.
VIOLA Also, people here see all those who come back to settle as wanting to change up their

	local homeland. Mostly, they try to recreate the foreign environment they come from here, instead of re-settling in Caribbean-style, among us. It's what people say, eh.
DENNIS	*(very attentive)* But there are divisions between people in the world, naturally; just as you find here or elsewhere.
ASHLEY	More than that, Dennis. In my view, I'm afraid migration has created a *THEM* and *US* cultural dichotomy within the Caribbean.
VIOLA	*(shrugs her shoulders)* You know, to be fair to those here eh, it's because the ones who come back here from abroad, create an imported class-system that just doesn't work here. *All ah we is one*, we used to say in the Caribbean; it's like some of them really forget that! The foreign-based nationals just come here to build up a big house, with fence so big, not even a fowl can pass, they don't give a thing to the local, so let's just say feelings are running high.
STACEY	You mean they're prejudiced against their own returning nationals, or is it vice versa?
ASHLEY	Let's just say, there's resentment on both sides, because some of those same returnees, spoil it for others. They come here and try to pull rank over the natives, by showing off on them, and acting like colonial masters, all over again. So, the people here think, *'Who the hell they think they are?'* and so on!
DENNIS	But I don't see why progress should bother anyone, as long as nobody's taking away

VIOLA anything from them. Y'know, I'd say it's difficult, even impossible, to stop progressive ideas from happening. You must know the saying, *'Time changes and so must men!'*

VIOLA My dear, it depends, but please, don't pay them no mind. Didn't you say you have access to all types of land equipment and strong links to business people in America who can help you?

DENNIS Yep, that I do. Y'know, Uncle Ash, I remember one day, when dad was trying to get me to be interested in the Caribbean. He suggested that with my qualifications, I could monopolise growth and development of land here, and rake in millions of dollars, if I wanted to. But at the time, I was just too stubborn and arrogant to understand that he was way ahead of the times.

ASHLEY Okay, but it's never too late, Dennis. You can quickly develop and expand yourself with good business help from here and also from over there, in America, as you say.

DENNIS Uh huh! And I think that *Time* will be the better arbiter of my plans for this place.

ASHLEY *(looks at his watch then stands)* And excuse the pun, but *Time also flies*, so we'll be heading home now before it gets dark. *(shaking Dennis' hands)* Take care, eh. *(shakes Stacey's hand)* Young lady, we'll catch up soon.

VIOLA *(hugs Dennis then Stacey)* Bye-bye, for now.

[Exit]

2:2 PAPA BOIS: KING OF PARADISE

Dennis and Stacey move onto a two-seater settee, sitting closely, eating treats from a tray.

DENNIS *(laughing)* Well, wasn't it hilarious? I mean, our two-way discussion?

STACEY I'm sure we were all definitely speaking about the future, but at cross-purposes!

DENNIS Well, we were talking about business with them, right? But as you know Stace, my ideas for expansion and growth here in this island is not the kind of business they're thinking about. So, yes, I'd say, we'll just have to wait and see how things pan out, once I start making some very big changes around here.

STACEY D, the kind of plans we were talking about last night, according to your aunt and uncle, would definitely brand us the "foreign-based or foreigners" that folks around here would definitely be wary of.

DENNIS Sure, and it was good to hear about the kinds of contentions that exist here among the people here; especially those they see as a threat, coming to change their way of life.

STACEY And with all the superstitions among the people, we could definitely be heading for a showdown!

DENNIS *(Stands, goes to a fridge)* Hah! *Papa Bois*, indeed! STUPES! *(sucks his teeth)* That's just old folks stories and tales about backwardness from plantation life. We're in the 20th century, and as far as I'm concerned, we have to move with the times.

2:2   PAPA BOIS: KING OF PARADISE

	(offers her a drink) Would you like another?
STACEY	Yes please!
DENNIS	*(smugly)* Besides, *my* kind of business will be bringing in money into this island, and helping to modernise their thinking and line their pockets. They should be glad for it.
STACEY	Honey, we'll just have to wait and see what transpires! I have a hunch there'll be some real battles ahead, though!
DENNIS	*(grinning mischievously, he opens a can of beer)* Yes, and I'm so ready for them!

[Curtains]

ACT 2 SCENE 3 - *GRAVE CONCERNS*

Ashley and Viola are at home. A meeting, instigated by the village priest, Rev. Truman, and three local Elders, (Egbert, Isaac, and Itran) are in progress. The Discussion is about Dennis' marijuana growing and manufacturing plans for his estate, and the increasing concerns in the locality. They are all sitting around a table.

ASHLEY	*(standing)* OK everyone, let me start our little gathering by thanking all-you for coming to our home to talk in a civil manner, about the grave concerns you have about my nephew. I really appreciate your coming here, to see if we can all find some agreeable solutions to put to Dennis, before things get out of hand. So I hand you over to the Reverend to lead us in a little prayer first.
REV. TRUMAN	*(he stands)* Well Papa Gawd, you said where two or three are gathered, you are in the midst to bless, so we ask you to bless us with the best possible solution and outcome for this big problem we face, right here in this village; in Jesus name.
EVERYONE	Amen!
REV TRUMAN	So I call on Egbert as the village Elder, to open the discussion.
EGBERT	Well, I guess I hardly have to tell all-you that there's big talk in the village about Ashley's nephew Dennis, hirin' young people like mad, and offerin' them big money to cut down absolutely everythin' on his entire 10-acre estate. He already brought in all kinds

EGBERT	of equipment from America, and even brought in some American workers!
ITRAN	What! Already? What's wrong with workers here?
EGBERT	Well, he's clearin' every single tree and bushes on the estate and turnin' it into a waste land. And do you know what for? To make way for a marijuana estate, where he'll cultivate marijuana and trade in its by-products! The bwoy also plan to build a hotel complex, quarters for sex workers, a brothel, and an entertainment club.
ISAAC	*(shaking his head)* Sacrilegious! He cyan come here and do that! You cyan cut down the trees in *Papa Bois* forest, for one. It's like runnin' *Papa Bois* away from the land, after all these past generations upon generations, we been followin' the tradition without trouble.
ITRAN	Now, you tell me how that young scrap of a bwoy come all the way from America, to come right here, to do this damn t'ing, eh! Ah doh need to tell all-you about the legend; I believe our *Papa Bois'* not going to let that happen; no siree!
ISAAC	The sad thing is, we've never ever had to confront *Papa Bois* in this land, before! Seems dis young Johnnie-come-lately, is openly disrespectin' our culture and disrespectin' each one of us, in the bargain, too!
ITRAN	Well, Ashley, if I didn' know it's your nephew, I'd go over there and give him a good hiding

	meself, to knock some sense into that bwoy's stubborn head, till he learn to show respect to the older heads in this place. We may look poor to him, but we have morals and dignity, and we're older and wiser than him.
ASHLEY	I hear you, but please, we mustn' take the law into our own hands. As a retired teacher, I'd always caution against any violence and instead, let's find an amicable solution for all concerned. We must lead by example, for the much younger ones.
REV. TRUMAN	Me too, I believe we mustn' follow the an-eye-for-an-eye principle, but at the same time, the young man needs to listen to what we have to say. So far, he refused to speak civilly to anyone, saying we're all backward, and talking plantation superstitious stories, about some folktale!
ITRAN	They better don't play with *Papa Bois*! Superstition? Huh, that's real foreigners' ignorance, for you!
REV TRUMAN	You see what I'm saying, they come over from their big overseas cities abroad, and think they better than us – bringing in their foreign ideas here and trying to tell us ours is backward! I say it's them who's backward, not us, for not understanding our folk culture, traditions, peoples way of life, and our history!
EGBERT	You're right, Rev! On top of that, every mother in this village is worried about her child or children associatin' with Dennis, his marijuana estate, and temptin' them with

	money. They say they're afraid that his attractive money and employment offers for youngsters to join him, will steal not only their minds and bodies, but also their souls. So they've already branded him an *"undesirable,"* among us.
ITRAN	And we know what *that* means! The last *"undesirable"* I can think of, was that fast-talkin' man from England, who came here with his BIG ideas, and opened up what he said was a Night Club on the beach; under the pretext of somethin' much nastier going on. Then one t'ing led to another, and just like that, he died in mysterious circumstances, and couldn't find his body for days!
REV. TRUMAN	Well, let's not forget the power of prayer too, eh. Who can blame parents for their worries and concern? From what you say he's planning to do; I believe Dennis' work is the work of the devil. It's right here, on our doorstep, and we have to root it out before it has a strong-hold. One solution is, my church will fast and pray, then we will find solutions of how to deal with that devil.
ASHLEY	I don't know how you'll do that, Rev. Because ah done talk and talk, till my mouth tired; the boy just won't listen. He's hell-bent on establishing a factory to cultivate and manufacture marijuana products on the estate. I have to tell all-you he showed me the plans – he's planning to build a brothel or strip club; acres and acres of propagators, for

REV TRUMAN	growing and cultivating marijuana; a small manufacturing plant; living quarters for workers; transport system for workers and guests. *(shakes his head)*
REV TRUMAN	*(looks upwards)* Papa Gawd, please help us!
ASHLEY	And the irony is, the boy claims he's creating employment to help the people here, because we can't do it ourselves. And because of that, he say we shouldn't be going against his plans. And guess what? They already put up a sign at the entrance gates to the estate, calling it *Paradise*!
ITRAN	What does he mean by sayin' we shouldn't go against his plans, eh? Who the hell this little up-start think he is? *Paradise*? What kinda *Paradise*, is it, and for who? STUPES!!
ASHLEY	Well, according to him, he's increasing our tourism economy, because people will be coming to spend their money here. I gather he's even going to provide free transport from the airport to the estate, hotel apartments for guests to stay! What irritates me is that Dennis seems to have thought up an answer for every damn question I have!
VIOLA	*(enters with food on a tray)* Excuse me for intruding gentlemen, but all that talking, I say all-you must be very hungry now. So, I brought some nice chicken and rice and peas. *(pointing to a sideboard)* Here is the ice-bucket - the mango juice drink is over there, please help yourself.

[Exits]

2:3 PAPA BOIS: KING OF PARADISE

ISAAC What that bwoy don't know is, there's talk about a local group of men who already form themselves into a gang and plannin' to attack Dennis soon, to frighten him. In fact, I hear that some men are sharpenin' cutlass, knives, sticks, machetes, bull-pistols, axes, swords, and all kinda things, for the surprise attack. They call themselves the *Mongoose Gang* and they bad like hell. So it seems war's comin'!

EGBERT Well, yes, sounds like war for true, because ah hear Dennis also have his own gang set-up here, a long time ago.

ISAAC Eh heh, wha' you sayin'?

EGBERT Well, why d'you think he brought all those American young scruffs here? They're not ordinary workers, ah hear they're really American gangsters, called *The Possum*!

REV TRUMAN *(looks upwards)* Lawd help us! First, we have this crazy young man calling himself *King of Paradise*, now we have *Mongoose* and *Possum* gangs clashing in this little place? Then, everything go really turn ole mass!

ASHLEY OK, OK, let's not be overwhelmed by this. What about getting Mr. Malone to speak to him. He's a respected local man in government, if anyone can have some sensible sway over the boy, it would be Malone.

ITRAN At this crucial time, we really don't have a choice. So let's get Malone!

2:3   PAPA BOIS: KING OF PARADISE

EGBERT   Wait! Did you say Malone! You jokin'? That Dennis done have Malone on his side already! In fact, he bribed a few other politicians, on both sides of the parties, and that's why there isn't any official opposition to his construction plans.

ITRAN   So you see, it seems that money does really talk!

EGBERT   Well yes, because if it was anyone one of us around here who dare to come up with such a scheme; man, those plans would ah never see the daylight, let alone pass the Planning Committee!

REV TRUMAN   So you saying it looks like we run into a brick wall, then. *(looks skywards)* But I still believe Papa Gawd have a plan and that plan would be on our side.

ISAAC   Eh heh! And don't forget we have Papa Bois; he is on our side too.

EGBERT   I would say we need a miracle, and the help of a local Newspaper on our side.

ITRAN   A newspaper? Tell me how they goin' to stop him? *(sniggers)* And that's if Dennis don't buy them yet!

EGBERT   Look man, we have to try everythin'. This is our homeland, and *Massa day done* long time ago; so the fight is on, with this young foreign *wanna-be* colonial. We done pass the stage when the white man come here, all the way from the other side of the world to build his empire, take over our land, and then turn all our people into slaves.

ITRAN   Man, I say, we done pass that stage! I say we should go in hard, and not treat Dennis with kid's glove. This softly, softly, approach, doh work!

EGBERT   Look, violence doesn't always solve anythin'. But right now, the whole damn t'ing is laughable, because it's our very own people who right now want to act as colonial masters; STUPES! That kinda imitation is a really a bad t'ing, for sure!

ASHLEY   OK, but we cyan give up now, so I'll try and continue to talk to my nephew and convey very strongly, all of your concerns. Leh we try in our individual ways, to make the boy see some sense, because compared to us, he's still only a young man. Why don't we meet up here again in a week, to feedback. Reverend, you agree?

REV TRUMAN   Well, alright! But I say let's all put this problem in very strong prayer too, because I believe, prayer changes things; the Bible says it can move mountains, so yes, leh we meet up again next week.

[Curtains]

ACT 2 SCENE 4 – *GANGSTERS & GREEDY MEN*

Dennis is at home in one of his Bars, with his closest Aides: Zack, Ed and Stan. They're discussing their plans to outsmart the enemy gang members and local dissenters of their project.

DENNIS	So Zack, what's the word out there, on the street? They still planning to cut off my neck? *(pokes fun, pretending to be afraid)* Oh, I'm so scared of *Papa Bois*! *(laughing, he runs around hilariously to laughter from the others).*
ZACK	*(laughs)* You-all should know the only word on the street is *our* word. *(cockily struts and beats his chest).* *Possum* is the word. We say what it means, and that's, "Shut your mouth if you want to live!"
ED	Yeah, and I checked with my boy Stan. He's got guys around the perimeter-fence day and night. Each man carrying a *strap*, and I hear *Mongoose* gang plan to show up any day now.
STAN	*(pulls out a plan, and points)* Look, I got some look-outs at the gates, over at this point, *here*. They walk in pairs *there*, and also along the road *here*, leading onto the estate, camouflaged as workmen. They all holding walkie-talkies; each man armed with a *strap*.
ZACK	We booby-trapped the fence around your house. *(grinning)* Electrified it 3000 volts, lethal! Anyone steps through *Paradise* Estate fence will, fry like a little fly! *(he

	mimics, taking out his gun inside his trousers) Zap! Zap! *(Pretends to blow out smoke from his gun).* One way in, definitely no way out! *(the others applaud)*
DENNIS	What about our spy inside *Mongoose* gang? What's happening there?
ZACK	Our King-pin there is Mark. He's spying on *Mongoose* gang for us! *(Shrugs)* Well, they don't pay their gang members and believe me when I tell you we pay Mark well; the guy's so happy he's willing to die for us, man!
STAN	Let's just say he's got good incentives to pretend to be a *Mongoose* member, for us! *(laughs loudly)*
DENNIS	Sounding good, guys. I like it. So, we get to know every step of their plans; even before they put them into action. *(motions them to come forward)* OK, but listen up! *(looks cautiously around, then whispers)* So, we have a big shipment coming in tomorrow mid-day; 25 Big-Shot Visitors, from the airport. These are heavy-duty dudes, treat them well.
ZACK	I'm on it, boss.
DENNIS	Meet them, get them up here safely to sample our products. Each one is a King-pin for us, on the outside of this place. They're our presence in the outside world. For extra safety, get more security to follow the pick-up from the airport.
STAN	I'm on it, boss.
DENNIS	Ed, go and see Stacey. Tell her we need some nice-looking girls tomorrow - the best.

	And Ed, work with Stacey on this. Our guests must have the best time of their lives, so they'll want to keep coming back for more and more.
ED	I'm on it too, boss.
DENNIS	*(rubbing his hands together)* In the meantime, I've got some more greasing palm to do; sucking in more greedy politicians from both sides. Imagine that! They're all competing to take my "dirty" money. *(laughing)* Damn Idiots!
ED	That's real cool, boss.
DENNIS	With them in our pockets, fellas! Who can stop our plans now? *(laughs loudly, they imitate by laughing also).*
STAN	I'll increase the boys around the gates, many will be camouflaged around the perimeter fence.
DENNIS	One last job. Get Ricky to gather a few of our men to lead some raids on the local village tonight, so they won't feel like coming out tomorrow! Understand, y'all need to rough up a few people, and ah mean really rough them up!
ZACK	*(cheeky laughs)* I distinctly heard you say break a few legs, and spill some blood, right boss!
DENNIS	Damn Zack! You heard me right! Find one or two local villagers on our side and splash the cash around. Give money publicly, and you'll always get greedy and very obedient volunteers!

2:4   PAPA BOIS: KING OF PARADISE

STAN *(he grins)* And we'll promise to offer them more, if they can tell us who's against us, right boss?

DENNIS Yeah, go out there and put the greedy confused cats among the even more greedy confused pigeons. That'll buy us hassle-free time tomorrow, whilst our guests sneak into the estate without notice.

ZACK Do we need ID details to collect them from the airport? Although coming from the United States, they shouldn't have any trouble clearing Customs.

DENNIS No, I got my *Homie* in Customs, he'll be taking care of our guests' clearance. He'll bring them to the pick-up area and from there you're in control and in charge of the smooth journey here, to me at the *Paradise mansion*, safely. *(He grins, waving his hand regally in the direction of the 6-bedroomed Great House).*

ZACK *(jokingly)* I'll be bringing them to Your Highness, the *King of Paradise*! *(bows low and the others laughing, imitate Zack; simultaneously, Dennis's phone rings)*

DENNIS *(answers phone)* Yagga Yow! Que passa? *(motions for the others to leave, then lowers his voice to a whisper)* I don't wanna hear he's still alive after the weekend! If you have to, find his entire family, and make every one of them disappear. That way you'll flush him out! *(spits, then with clenched teeth)* And Jamal, I say, make it look like an accident! You and Sammy, only talk to me again when

2:4   PAPA BOIS: KING OF PARADISE

it's all over. *(angrily, spits in disgust)* You've got till Friday!

[Curtains]

ACT 2 SCENE 5 – *SCHEMES GO AWRY*

Jeeps with VIP guests and their Drivers are surprisingly waylaid on the Estate lands, en route from the airport to Paradise Estate Great House, by other unexpected, non-human 'guests'!

ZACK   *(on walkie-talkie)* Come in Stan, it's me Zack! Mission VIP, Stan, it's me Zack. Over!

STAN   Radio check, Zack, you got the all-clear to approach the gates. Over!

ZACK   Come in. You kidding me, right now! How did you let all those animals get inside the grounds. Look, got no time to waste right now. You had one little job to increase manpower and electrify perimeter fence. Over.

STAN   Negative. What you talking about, man? What animals, we aint got no animals on this estate! Over.

ZACK   Say again. Then tell me what the hell is this! Right now, there's about 50 animals surrounding our jeeps! If this is some kinda game, now's not the right time to play it, man. You heard Dennis yesterday, so you need to help me get into the entrance gates. Over.

STAN   Negative. Man you not making sense at all. You been sampling the *gear*? You know we have strict orders not to touch the merchandise. Right now, you're sounding like you're high to me. Stand by.

ZACK   Wait, wait up! What the ....! There's a flipping old, ragged man, like some sort of tramp sanding with them. Where the hell did he come from? Over!

STAN	Come in. What man, where's he at? No one can come through the perimeter with 3000 voltages, not a single man or animal. Over.
ZACK	Repeat. Well, unless my eyes deceiving me, he's standing a little distance away, just staring at us, with all these animals gathered around our jeeps. Over.
STAN	Negative. You freaking me out, man. What about the guests? Over.
ZACK	Stand by. They're inside the jeeps, I just told them to hang on, while I shush the animals out of the way. The bloody animals not budging, so I climbed out and that's when I see the old dude. He's like a tramp, with leaves in his hair, just staring me down, without saying a word. Over.
STAN	Copy. I'll get some men down to you right away. They'll be on their way now. Over, and out!
ZACK	*(turns around to the stranger)* Hey, mister, what's your name and how come you get in here with all these animals? *(no response, Zack pulls out his gun and points at the stranger)* Listen buster, you got one minute to get out of here with these animals, or you will be sorry. *(takes aim with his gun)* Don't force me to use this weapon, 'cos I will.
STAN	Come in Zack, you there? Over!
ZACK	Roger. Course, I'm here, told you I can't go anywhere! Over.
STAN	Ten four. OK got three men on their way to you right now, over. Confirm the situation there now. Over!
ZACK	*(10 minutes later)* Come in Stan. Over.
STAN	Copy. Loud and clear. Over.
ZACK	Look man, no more promises. It's been more than 10 minutes, no back-up's here, what y'all playing at? The Boss won't be pleased to hear this. Over.

STAN	Copy. Who says he needs to know about this? Over.
ZACK	Look, I'm trying to handle this situation, so it won't be necessary for him to question the safety of his guests and merchandise. Over.
STAN	Affirmative. Back-up should've been with you by now, three men with *straps*. Over.
ZACK	Negative. There's no show, and time's ticking. Over.
STAN	Copy. I need an update on their whereabouts, will get back to you. Over and out.
ZACK	*(turns around to address the stranger)* Hey, mis...ter.....! Where the hell did he go? *(a horn is heard blowing, the animals follow the direction of the sound, they disappear, as instantly as they came).*
STAN	Come in, Zack. I can't seem to be able to get hold of anybody right now. Don't know what the hell's going on. These men should've been with you ten minutes ago. Over.
ZACK	Break, break. Listen man, the animals and the old geezer's just disappeared! Over.
STAN	Come in! Sorry man, this is too freaky. You say the animals disappeared and the old hobo disappeared too, without saying anything? Over.
ZACK	Affirmative. I just turned my back to call you and zoom, they gone! The hairs on my head are on end. This is some freak show, man! Got to get back in the jeep and head out. Over.
STAN	Copy. Let's keep this on the down-low, till we check it out, something's not right. Over.
ZACK	Affirmative. Say no more, it's too freaky to explain. Don't want Dennis thinking the place is not secure, especially now, when we need security the most. Over.

2:5   PAPA BOIS: KING OF PARADISE

STAN   Affirmative. You're right, and with no back-up reaching you, even as we speak, tells me something really strange is going on man, and I don't like it. For all I know, we could all be in for it. Over.

ZACK   *(looks at his watch)* Roger. But leh me go now. Got to get those people over to Dennis, pronto. We'll talk about this later, just you and me. I mean, no one would believe us anyway, right? Over.

STAN   Affirmative. We'll talk later. And like I said, keep it on the down-low, till we know what the hell's really going on. Over and out!

[Curtains]

ACT 3 SCENE 1 - *THE DILEMMA!*

In a local Barber shop. Two Barbers and their clients are discussing the pros and cons of Dennis' marijuana enterprise.

BARBER 1	Tell me Reggie, ah hear you workin' with all those people who're livin' it up in *Paradise*. So, wha' really happenin' down dere, bwoy?
REGGIE	Well, is a lot ah t'ings happenin', but as for me, my job is inside the propagators; makin' sure the workers don't steal the products. My boss payin' them for their work, and that's all.
BARBER 1	What you sayin'? *(shaking his head)* Ah doh understand wha' you mean!
REGGIE	Well, take for instance, all workers who packagin' the marijuana products, have to work naked. That's to make sure they don't hide things on them or inside of them, and divert Dennis' trade to their little side-hustle.
BARBER 1	What! Lawd have mercy! So, who's doin' de packagin'?
REGGIE	Women mostly, and before you criticise eh, they happy to get $100 US at the end of the week. Because, If they just sit down home with no work, tell me who go just give them $100 for nothin'?
BARBER 1	So you mean to tell me, all-you young people, lose your blasted souls to Dennis-the-Devil, for $100 a week. Isn't dat what everyone callin' him around here, a devil?
REGGIE	*(half-laughing)* Look, we not sufferin' anybody. It's workin' you know, just like

	harvestin' cocoa and banana. It's just a different product, that's all, but it's doin' an honest day's work and gettin' paid for it.
BARBER 2	And where's the dignity in this kinda workin' naked, just so a man can pocket all the money? He makin' all-you work like it's slavery days all over again; only this time, every one of you volunteered to be slaves.
BARBER 1	Yeah man, dis Dennis is sure imitatin' colonialism. De man come here takin' advantage of people's lack of money, engage in illegal trade, plantin' and harvestin' drugs, splashin' his cash around to fool all-you, and every one of you fall for it!
REGGIE	With all respect eh, if ah didn't know better, I would say all-you against Dennis because he have money. Look around you, at least young people are now doin' somethin' for themselves right inside that man's estate. They're employed, and they gettin' paid for what they do.
BARBER 2	Gettin' paid to lose their dignity? STUPES! Taking the Yankee dollar, and losin' their souls.
REGGIE	Well, what all-you prefer they do? Sit around rum shops, lazin' about on verandas and slappin' sand-flies, or runnin' behind young gals, or makin' children, without knowin' how they go feed them?
BARBER 1	So you sayin' tradin' your soul with de devil for bread, is a better way of livin'? Listen, eh, all old people in dis country know how to make do with little. Small as it was, dey did

3:1 PAPA BOIS: KING OF PARADISE

bring up all of you youngsters in a decent way; to make sure all-you get ah education to better yourselves, and you tellin' me now it amount to growin' ganga and employin' naked women?

BARBER 2   That's a good question! Young people these days need to think long and hard about the kind of world they want for their children. Otherwise, look at how easy it is for a foreigner, to come here, right under our noses and make them trade their dignity, culture, tradition, and land, for quick dirty schemes that can't sustain the land or the generations to come.

BARBER 1   It's true man! Because we can't eat marijuana to live, but plantin' cocoa, banana, nutmeg, breadfruit, yam, and sweet potatoes can make sure all our families can stay alive for de rest of our lives; just as our people did in de past. We must respect de land, because it can outlast every one of us, and every stupid scheme!

REGGIE   Look, don't get me wrong, eh; I understand whe' you comin' from, but right now, there is a need, and people thinkin' about puttin' food on their tables to feed their children every day.

MIKEY   Fellas, leh me jump in right here, because ah been stayin' quiet, listenin' to all-you long enough. De way I see it eh, we have to blame our own politicians, who allow foreigners to just walk into our country and do as dey damn well please.

3:1   PAPA BOIS: KING OF PARADISE

BARBER 2   *Now* you talkin' man! Speak!

MIKEY   Well yes, look at de Chinaman and his technology, de Japanese with their cars, de Englishman with his Buckingham Palace, and de U.S.A. with their White House. Tell me, which one of dem would have any one of us just breeze into their country and say we plantin' ganga, bringin' in tourists freely from de airport, payin' off people to keep dem quietly sufferin' their own people dis way! I say no-way they will let dat happen to dem!

BARBER 1   Den, in dat case, we have to say dat our politicians are failin' our young people. It's a fact, dey takin' bribes themselves; secretly acceptin' dirty money, and turnin' a blind eye to de evil goin' on right under their noses. So, because we're not stoppin' it, we are encouragin' it; you could say we are powerless, and have to suffer because of dat.

ALAN   But all-you forgettin', de Chinaman is right here, in dis country too, lookin' for land to settle his ever-growin' population, so why not Dennis; especially as Paradise Estate is *his very own* piece of land) He didn' take from anybody!

BARBER 2   Look eh, Japanese making cars, because people globally will always want cars; so, it's a future for their nation. As for the Englishman, well he done colonise everybody and take the best they had; so now he sittin' pretty, and at the same time he re-packagin' our very own t'ings and sellin' it back to us.

3:1 PAPA BOIS: KING OF PARADISE

BARBER 1 So, are you sayin' Dennis is justified in what he doin'; exploitin' his own kind for what? Let's not repeat past mistakes. Because he's black, it doh mean we have to be soft with him. It's still de same exploitation - takin' advantage of poor people, while our weak governments pocketin' de benefits. Didn't dey say, *Massa Day done*, but look how it come back to haunt us; way down de line! Man, I say we should be ashamed to call ourselves an independent country!

ALAN Preach brother! De thing is, when we realise dat trauma stems from trauma, den we'll put a stop to dis foolishness and protect our future generations. But how dat will happen for real? Man, I really, don't know!

MIKEY Dat's not all, eh. Before we know it, these big, dirty, stray-men will be breedin' our young girls, spreadin' sexual diseases, and wouldn't have de time of day for a single victim they'll leave behind.

BARBER 1 Yeah man, it's just as the Mighty Sparrow calypso said, way back then; *"When you catch them broken, you catching them all for nothing."* He mean poor, hungry people willin' to sell their bodies for a few dollars or next to nothin' to de Yankee man, because they're broke like hell!

MIKEY So, as before, de consequence is, *we* are de ones left with the casualties. Tell me if dat isn't a different kind of colonialism by Dennis; and a black man too! Rape, pillage, exploitation, degradation, manipulation,

	deceit, covetousness. Look, doh get me rile today, eh. I say, we have to run dis good-for-nothin' out of our island - dat's for sure!
LESLIE	I agree, we need a revolution in dis land, for people to wake up to de reality of all these wolves in sheep clothin', comin' to steal our children's birth-right and future, all over again.
MIKEY	Ok, all-you grand-standing, but which one of our leaders go do dat? I mean, who will lead a revolution and speak for us?
	(there's silence)
LESLIE	You see, dis silence right here? Now, dat's exactly what's happenin' everywhere in dis land. Don't forget dey say a people without a voice, is like lambs to de slaughter.
MIKEY	We must claim our voice back and speak loud-loud, about what's happenin'; in case our silence give de impression we agree with de wrong. Because history shows dat sometimes changes only come when brave men stand up and speak against injustice, and fight against it, if dey have to.
LESLIE	It's true, every single rebel's first step to freedom, start with his voice, spreadin' de word and mobilisin' support.
BARBER 1	Ah hear you!
MIKEY	Dat's why I'm invitin' all-you to ah open-air meetin', behind Charlie rum-shop on Saturday night, to talk about these things.
BARBER 1	Well yes, I will come, because if war's goin' to come to our streets, we need to be leadin' de charge, and not be bystanders.

BARBER 2 *(carefully cutting)* Mikey, hold you head steady, you sweatin' like a pig with all this anger. Hold still man, before you make me cut you so people will say I'm a bad barber.

MIKEY OK, OK, but somebody have to speak up for us, and as for me, I'm not afraid to speak, eh! Either we speak up or shut up, and take our trouble quietly, like cat got our tongues.

BARBER 2 Calm down man, you can't do it all by yourself. I hear the village *Mongoose* gang plannin' to pay Dennis a visit soon. And Reggie, ah doh mind sayin' it aloud, because it's not a secret. Even you know that Dennis, your boss, have an American gang right here too, isn't that right?

REGGIE Well, all I will say is, they better know that we won't be jokin' when they come. In fact, Dennis' *Possum* gang will be waitin' for them.

BARBER 2 So, wait, you mean to tell me, all-you really have a gang called *Possum* here in this country a'ready? *(stops cutting his client's hair, waves his hand)* Look at me ass cross, noh! You see, all these foreign bad habits; idiots with guns runnin' riot in our streets, is not our way of life. Now their killin' trend come to take hold of our people, on our very streets! We have young children who will witness this damn stupidness and before you know it, they will think it's cool and start to imitate killin' too.

REGGIE Look, it's not as bad as it sounds, trust me. Yes, it's true things are different but not as bad as you put it. Plus, Dennis plans are goin' to happen anyway, because he already have the plannin' permission to go ahead with his construction - the hotel apartments, Night Club, and a host of other things; so it really looks like *all systems go what's planned*!

MIKEY Huh! Dat wicked den of iniquity, his own Sodom and Gomorrah, just like Jericho in de Bible, dis wall will come tumblin' down, because nothin' so evil and damagin' to young souls, will last forever. *(looking skywards)* Papa Gawd, you're in charge!

BARBER 2 *(showing Mikey the mirror and brushing the excess hair from his shoulders)* I'd say you have a master hair cut today, despite wrigglin' all over de place with all dat grand-charge and loud-loud talkin'.

MIKEY *(paying him)* T'anks my brother, *(looks in the mirror)* Woo-ee! Eh-eh, ah lookin' good, man! *(brushes off remnants of cut hairs and addresses the others)* Look man, a person have to get t'ings off his chest, and speak his mind to other men. Where else can we do dat?

BARBER 1 I'll tell you where - only here - in **Sam's Barber Shop**; and remember, there's always a place here to discuss and put de world to right. *(addresses the group)* Look man, we're doin' better talkin' here, dan all of dem politicians put together in dat Parliament buildin', because in dis place, *real* men talk *real* truth; without fear of revenge. *(moves*

3:1   PAPA BOIS: KING OF PARADISE

towards Reggie with hand outstretched) So, Reggie, no hard feelin's, eh!

REGGIE *(shaking hands)* Well, they say old men talk wisdom, young men fight hastily, and so I listened to all of your wisdom today. I get whe' you comin' from, and I respect dat, but my opinion's still de same. *(gestures love and solidarity, by touching his heart with his fist)* But, I leave all-you in peace brothers, no hard feelin's eh; ah have to go now.

[Exits]

MIKEY *(calls out after him)* Still, don't forget to come on Saturday, eh; behind Charlie Rum Shop! Six o'clock!

BARBER 2 *(waves)* Take it easy man; we go catch up soon.

[Curtains]

ACT 3 SCENE 2 – *MAKING SUPPLICATIONS*

In a church meeting, three of Dennis' Paradise workers are introspectively responding to Rev. Truman's sermon against Dennis' illegal drug development and gang violence on the island.

REV. TRUMAN (*Standing in front of a seated congregation*) And now, before we take the communion, let's put our burdens to Gawd, and pray very hard against this cancerous problem that has taken root in our village. This disease is no other than that den of iniquity, that cell of debauchery, that destroyer of young lives; led by the devil's agent, in our very own country, in the form of *Paradise* Estate owner, Dennis, and his development.

CHURCH Amen!

REV TRUMAN It's our responsibility to the little ones in our midst, that we always speak against any evil that threatens their lives.

CHURCH Amen!

IVY **[Aside]:** (*stands*) Papa Gawd, I know it's wrong what's goin' on in *Paradise* Estate, and I must confess, I work there. I see the wrong-doings they talkin' about, but who go feed my children if I leave? This is my first piece of paid work in years. I can save a little, send Alan to school, buy his school uniforms, shoes, and school books. At leas' now, we can eat decent food, without dependin' on the goodness of someone's heart for hand-outs, or from stray men,

	lookin' for a place to lay down their hats. *(sits down)*
REV TRUMAN	This little village, a peaceful place from as long as any of us can remember, has become the scene of violent gang warfare on our streets. As you know, only last week, we were all under curfew from 6pm to 6am because gangs – *Mongoose* and *Possum* – are running our very own streets.
CHURCH	No more, Lawd!
REV TRUMAN	They're fighting with guns imported here, to kill our children; who, before now, wouldn't dare handle a gun because they didn't have a gun! Now that evil has taken hold of them, they can look at another woman's child, point a gun at him, pull the trigger and easily take his life; as if it means nothing!
CHURCH	Lawd, help us!
NELLY	*[Aside]: (stands)* Papa Gawd, why can't a person work in peace? I don't have anyone to depend on, and quite frankly, even though I have to work in my pantie and bra, it's better than someone wantin' to take what's inside them, and leave me hungry and pregnant! Papa Gawd, forgive me, for workin' naked but I honestly believe I'm not doing anythin' wrong. *(sits down)*
REV TRUMAN	Only two days ago, two mothers lost their teenage sons, to gang war-fare on our streets; right here in our little village! We are all shocked by such news and the increasingly shocking, daily, newspaper

	headlines these days. We are pained for all grieving families.
CHURCH	We feel pain! Shame! Disgrace!
LYDIA	*[Aside]:* (*stands*) Gawd forgive me, but I did hear them talkin' about it in *Paradise Estate* and even boastin' about it too. Dennis' *Possum* gang kill a *Mongoose* gang member, but Papa Gawd, I'm tellin' you, workin' there doesn't mean I condone violence and the takin' of a life. Yes, I'm tormented by the killin', because my own son is a teenager too, and I grieve for that dead boy's mother. But the thing is, how we going to feed our families, without the competition, hatred, and corruption of these groups? It's not that I'm tradin' my morals, dignity, or anythin', but all I can say is, Papa Gawd, inside my heart, only you know the answer. (*sits down*)
REV TRUMAN	Church, only three weekends ago, a good politician, who was brave enough, spoke out against the corruption of his colleagues in taking bribes and the illegal development taking place at *Paradise Estate,* just disappeared. What happened to him? Since then, nobody's seen him. Some say he was kidnapped! Church, are we contented?
CHURCH	No! Help us, Lawd! Not contented!
REV TRUMAN	So, Brethren, what have we become? Fearful, gangsters, drug addicts, drug traffickers, murders, violent criminals? That's the work of the devil, and we must stand up against it, as men and women of

	God, otherwise we would not be doing the Lawd's work.
CHURCH	Amen! We stand against it!
GLORIA	*[Aside]:* *(stands)* Oh Lawd! I feel like my heart goin' to burst! *Paradise Estate* people did kidnap that poor politician. I know they're keepin' him in a basement somewhere on the Estate. I know that, but can I really tell anyone? No, ah doh want no trouble eh! Will that save him? Will it protect me, and what about my children, if they kill me? You see, this thing call a wall of silence, is worse than a knife, because it slicin' you open inside; every day, every time you think about the wrong-doin', that you should be exposin,' instead of hidin'. *(sits down)*
REV TRUMAN	Church! We must not be afraid. Remember, Jesus himself had to speak against the Sadducees and Pharisees, without fear. We too, must continue to speak against what's happening in our midst. It's an abomination, so we must pray and fast, and seek God's face for answers.
CHURCH	Speak! Preach! Amen!
ANNE	*[Aside]:* *(stands)* I feel like a fraud, comin' to church and hidin' the wrong by workin' at *Paradise Estate*, and no one here knows. My heart's tellin' me stop it and get out, but my head says, just carry on, as long as you don't open your big mouth, nobody will know. After all, you've done OK, so far, lookin' after

	yourself and children. May Gawd forgive me. *(sits down)*
REV TRUMAN	We must continue to pray against what's happening in our country because we believe that prayer changes things and it can move mountains. So, if anybody have anything they want prayer for, now's the time to come up to the front, and the prayer team will come and assist.
SEEMA	*[Aside]: (stands)* Well, Papa Gawd, I don't need to go to the front and speak to any Prayer Team. I done talk to you already, so look out for me and my family, eh. I'm not an accomplice to the wrong-doin', I just want to feed my family. I promise I won't hurt anyone. *(sits down)*
REV TRUMAN	Anyone wish to come for prayer? *(pauses)* Just come forward, and speak to God, clear your consciences, cleanse your minds and your souls, as we are going to seek revelations, miracles, and solutions to all these problems in our village and country; especially the problem of the *Paradise Estate* development. They need deliverance, so we're going to pray for them. Anybody need prayer? Now is the time to come up front for prayer too!
LYDIA	*[Aside]: (stands)* Dear Gawd, I don't need the Prayer Team today. Although I would like to clear my conscience with all this knowledge of what's going on, I feel I've already done that, talkin' to you. I know by talkin' to these people, the exposure would

	put me and my family life in jeopardy. Please excuse me this time, Lawd. I'll help release the kidnapped politician, if I hear they intend to kill him. But if it comes to that, me and my children will need your protection from persecution. So, Papa Gawd, I'm relyin' on you. *(sits down)*
REV TRUMAN	Is there no one who needs prayer today?
VERNA	*[Aside]: (stands)* As for me, ah might as well go and ask God to forgive me for joinin' *Paradise Estate*. After all, I'm only 18 years old, my whole life's in front of me. Only last month, my aunt in America said she would send for me. Yes, it's time to get out of this place. I'm takin' my mother's advice, and goin' abroad to do better for myself, before it's too late. Yes, I'd better go up for prayer now. It'll clear my conscience, and help me to stop workin' in *Paradise Estate*, because it's my choice. Leh me go up for prayer now. *(hurries up the altar)*. All-you wait, ah comin'!
REV TRUMAN	Well then, Ushers, bring the communion trays after we pray for this young lady. I do believe that after our 21 days of fasting, the Lawd will deliver us from the evil that is in our country, Amen!
CHURCH	Amen!

[Curtains]

ACT 3 SCENE 3 – *MASSA DAY DONE!*

Outside Charlie's rum shop. Local men and women from the village and surrounding arears have gathered for an open-air meeting. They are protesting against their government's aiding and abetting of Dennis' illegal drug trade, immoral working conditions, unvetted building plans and general leniency with gang violence and warfare on the Streets; which have led to recent curfews.

MIKEY *(addresses a large crowd)* Brothers! Sisters! Brethren! You know yourself why every one of us is here today. It's not to weep over our current situation in dis country. It's not to lament over our current oppression from those we elect in government; those who now choose to dishonour us, disregard us, and treat us like *kunumoonoo!* It's to take swift action now!

CROWD *(chants loudly)* Dat's right! Time for action!

MIKEY We have been too contented in keepin' silent over recent events, and now's de time to break our silence. Some of you are bound by your participation in *Paradise Estate*; a place dat one man – a foreigner – has decided to use as a gulf between you and those who are supposed to be runnin' dis country. Dat place affects and persecutes you at de same time, givin' you fast money and hope in one hand and takin' away your dignity, moral freedom, and peace of mind and safety in our homes, with de other hand. Brothers and sisters, we have been oppressed before;

	our ancestors were slaves of all European colonizers, and we once said dat *Massa Day was Done*!
LESLIE	So, today we say again *Massa Day Done* a long time ago! We're not a free-for-all country. Dis is *our* country; where we have laws, and *everyone* should live by dem, not just some!
MIKEY	Well, as you know, dis isn't our first meetin'. We addressed many issues, mourned over your past sorrows; overcame in situations in dis land many of you thought were impossible. Dat same power of de voice, fightin' against the spirit of injustice, still burns in our hearts, brothers, and sisters. De Almighty Gawd has seen it fit to shine his light on us, so we are still here standin' up to what's wrong.
CROWD	Dat's right! Speak man!
MIKEY	Well, open all-you eyes and see de similarities with slavery all over again. Dis time, we seem to have a wolf in sheep's clothin'; a black man possessin' huge acres of land, behaving just like a coloniser. Den, he boldly bring over his 'bad dogs' (you know, I mean his street gangs), to keep us in check. Imagine that! Those American marauders are imported gangs, right here controllin' our streets, and secretly killin' our young ones. And what for?
LESLIE	To ply his illegal trade among our people, with 100% freedom to bring in drug lords in

MIKEY and out of our country, without government objection.

MIKEY Dat's right! And all-you remember what de old Massa did?

ITRAN He took our women, exploited dem, rape, disrespect, and den turn dem into slaves.

MIKEY Well, today, look for yourselves. What is Dennis, dat devil's agent, doin'? He, like de old coloniser, have your daughters, mothers, wives workin' naked for him, down to their panties and bras, while they process ganga products, somethin' dat is illegal in dis land. And who give him permission?

ITRAN Our very own politicians, our government! In fact, they let him bring in all kinds of kingpins, and drug lords into our country, from some of de worst countries in de world. Soon, de world will be sayin' we're no better dan some well-known drug tradin' places in South America!

MIKEY Dat's right, you and I have been betrayed. All-you know our history, so what are you goin' to do about it?

WOMAN 1 I agree we been betrayed. But all-you better be careful too, eh! Some people say dat because Preacher John was publicly campaignin' against *Paradise Estate*, de fire dat destroyed his church, last weekend, was a deliberate attack, to frighten, silence, and run him outa town.

AZACCA Brethren, Greetin's in the name of His Imperial Majesty, Emperor Haile Selassie, Jah Rastafari, who liveth and reigneth I'n'I

3:3 PAPA BOIS: KING OF PARADISE

	itinually, ever faithful, ever sure. I'n'I seh fiyah bun babylon kaaz dem eva dey tarment poor people.
CROWD	Babylon is a thief!
AZACCA	But hear noh, a lat a greedy betrayer 'tween us, jus' sittin pon dem backside saying Mi nuh hav nutten fi complain bout, mi life irie, but mek ah tell you sumthin', I'n'I come here to say, jus' like Bob Marley did, wi guh chase dem crazy ball head outta town - dat Dennis and hi *Possum* gang, who come here to grow and sell his genetically modified blodclart sinsemilla here.
CROWD	Chase dem out!
AZACCA	Dat Dennis is nat a real fiyah man, and dat thin' he sellin' is not de healin' herb we know. Jus' like everytime, babylon come to trick I'n'I wit him poison, so wen we turn fool-fool, den he tek over everythin'. But we haffi play fool fi ketch wise and trap him.
CROWD	*(from the crowd)* Trap him like manicou!
AZACCA	Mi nuh truss deh bredda deh, kaaz him a bag o wire. So, I'n'I and mi brethren standin' wit you. I'n'I waitin' to chase dat crazy ball head outta our yard. We go chase Dennis and de politicians outta our village, outta town and outta our island. Say wen, I'n'I, and mi brethren from the north, wi ready on standby! Nuff respect. *(salutes with a raised fist)* Jah!
CROWD	*(chants loudly with fists in the air)* Rastafari!
WOMAN 2	Well, look at me! A mother, and my heart breakin' for me only son. De boy get involve

3:3 PAPA BOIS: KING OF PARADISE

with dat *Paradise* Estate, and he takin' de drugs night and day! Now if you see him - his head not good at all! De child screamin' in de night, say he seein' little beasts and holdin' his head and bawlin'. We have no peace. All-you know is de ganga mixed with other drugs there dat killin' him, because before dis drugs estate existed, my son mind was straight as a dial. Now look at me arse cross! And not only dat! Children, who go to *Paradise* and taste de life there, are now fightin' parents and all kind ah mele goin' on right now in de place.

CROWD Down with dese Undesirables! Dey mus' go!

WOMAN 3 Don't forget dat bwoy Dennis have a lot of backing, eh. Even de Newspapers dat was once writin' against de damage to de environment, to de youths, and de failin' economy, suddenly started to change their tune! Look how happily they're now runnin' adverts for *Paradise Estate*? So you see, money does talk, and *Paradise Estate* money seems to be talkin' very loudly!

CROWD Is 'fraid, they 'fraid of revenge. But I'm not afraid though.

NOAH *(holds his hand up for calm and silence)* Well, listen eh, ah hear somethin' happen on de estate when de boys were bringin' over some kingpins and drug lords to de Estate. Nobody explainin' what really happen but one or two people were scared and there's only whisperin'; sayin' dat dey sure it must have somethin' to do with *Papa Bois*!

PAPA BOIS: KING OF PARADISE

ITRAN   You see, I knew it wasn't goin' to be long before *Papa Bois* showed up. Some people like to laugh and dismiss de old folk stories, but I have news for them. When I was only 14 years old, I saw *Papa Bois* in de forest with my own eyes. I was with my grandfather. He just appeared from thin air and stood there starin' at us, without sayin' one single word, then he disappeared, just as instantly as he did come.

NOAH   So what did he come for?

ITRAN   Well, quite a lot of us were huntin' wild meat and we did catch a good amount, everyone was celebratin'. In fact, we had enough, but it was a lucky day and dem fellas wanted more and more! Ah could hear in de distance a horn blowin and before you know it, de pig we were about to stake, turned and ran towards de sound of de horn – just like it was answerin' de call. In fact, all de animals dat day was runnin' towards de sound also; and there wasn't even one more left for us to catch.

NOAH   You mean you see him with your own eye?

ITRAN   Yeah man, just like I seein' you right now. So after dat day, my grandfather sat me down and told me de old story of *Papa Bois*. Some say he's not real, but believe me, he's real. He's one very serious lookin' fella, with leaves in in his hair, a bit thin, wild eyes, could frighten anybody. They say if you ever see him, you must be polite and don't look

3:3   PAPA BOIS: KING OF PARADISE

	him in the eyes. In fact, he is as hairy as any animal, and is usually only dressed In a pair of ragged trousers, with a horn in his belt.
MIKEY	So wait, you're sayin' this *Papa Bois* character exists as a person? I thought it was just a folktale old people used to tell at night.
ITRAN	Well, they say that de story of *Papa Bois* existin' is true. Not only dat, but they also say he can turn himself into a deer or any other animal with cloven hoofs, and has leaves growin' out of his beard. He may lead bad hunters into de forest, and reveal himself, in order to warm or force dem to comply with de conservation rules of de forest; den he vanishes.
MIKEY	Well, as for me, I always respect de older heads, so if an elderly person say so, den it must be so!
ITRAN	Yes, they say *Papa Bois* usually sound a horn to warn his friends, which are de animals, of hunters. Dat's because he doesn't tolerate killin' for killin's sake, or man's greed and destruction of de land. So when anybody see him, you know for sure he's really angry about somethin' we're doing to de land — and there'll be consequences too, eh.
NOAH	Oh-ho! So *now* I understand de *Papa Bois* story, because to tell de truth, I used to hear de name *Papa Bois,* but I never knew de full story. So, in dat case, you could say *Papa Bois* is just as angry as we are. Yes, it seems dat he's paying de *Paradise* boys a visit, for a good reason! Now dat I represent all those

	from de south, I can tell you we're ready when all-you ready to strike, eh.
ITRAN	Then, dat's good. It means everybody, even *Papa Bois,* is at war with *Paradise Estate* and those corrupt politicians who're breakin' de laws of dis land.
MIKEY	Well, dat's good. De fight is really happenin' on all fronts. And unless we resist, we will continue to be oppressed. *Resistance* is our motto. We refuse to be under de oppressors. Our ancestors didn't just submit to tyranny and give up, dey fought de spirit of de devil for years and eventually broke it. And because their blood runs in our veins, let's be awake, as their voices call us from their graves to strike; to strike while de iron's hot for justice. Just know dat every man, woman, and child from the east of de country is on standby, waitin' for de call.
CROWD	*(loud chants, with fists in the air)* Long live the Resistance! Leh we fight! Time to resist!
MIKEY	Brethren! Remember Toussaint Louverture, Nanny, Paul Bogle, and even Gang-Gang Sarah. Dey broke de movement of slavery and de slave empire; like dem, we breakin' dis modern-day slavery. Let's take up our machetes, bull-pistols, cutlass, axes, swords, whatever weapon you have, bring it. We go stamp out de evil, includin' those greedy, corrupt politicians; once and for all.
CROWD	*(loud chants, with fists in the air)* Do it now! No more waitin'! Do it now!

3:3   PAPA BOIS: KING OF PARADISE

MIKEY *(holds up his hands for silence)* Brothers and sisters, yes, you been patient long enough, so I say choose revolution today! Den we'll restore our peace and security in dis land. If you want to re-set de clock back to safety on our streets, let's fight to drive away de kingpins, drug-lords and gangsters from our country. Den we'll never forget those who enabled dis vile development from de west, to spread like a cancer from parish to parish in our country.

CROWD *(loud chants, with fists in the air)* Revo! Revo! Down with Dennis! Beast from the west!

MIKEY Listen eh, some of you may bleed, some of you may even die, but I say, it's better to bleed and die as heroes, standin' up for rights in our country, than to daily feel like you're bleedin' and dyin' inside your hearts; at de mercy of dese 'undesirables.'

CROWD *(several loud chants, with fists in the air)* We go bleed! We go die! We had enough! Down with de evil! Massa day done! Revolution!

MIKEY *(lowers voice into a whisper)* Brothers and sisters, come closer. Now, here's our battle-plan!

[Curtains]

ACT 3 SCENE 4 – *A LAST DITCH ATTEMPT*

Rev. Truman is meeting with Ashley and Viola in their home for a last ditch attempt to stop Dennis' Marijuana enterprise and the rising gang warfare spreading throughout the island.

REV TRUMAN	Good day, and thanks for seeing me one last time, to deal with this ever-growing problem with your nephew. Things seem like they really getting out of hand. There's a lot of rumour going around abut a revolution. And it's not sounding too good. So, I thought to myself, let the three of us make one last-ditch attempt to appeal to these young hot-heads before it's too late.
ASHLEY	Thanks for coming, Rev. We know it's our responsibility to help put things right. After all, we're the elders of this village, and Dennis is my blood. At the same time it's our duty to protect both young and old in this situation.
VIOLA	As for me, I feel very bad that my own nephew's head is so damn hard; no matter what we tell him. Somehow we can't seem to get through to him; it's like the devil really take 'e soul. At first, he listens but then laughs afterwards, saying he's doing more for the island than our rotten politicians, who're pocketing his money.
REV TRUMAN	*(shaking his head)* So what does Dennis really mean? He think he's our saviour? The boy's barely 30 years old, but thinks he can tell **us** what to do! *(shakes his head)* Ah doh know eh! This modern type of education

nowadays, doesn't seem to have enough good role-models to convince me that those who call themselves 'educated' are better than us old folks, or have the right to slight our wisdom. *(adds quickly)* And of course, we rely on the Lawd; by praying and fasting, to guide us.

ASHLEY   I know Rev, I know; humility is a good virtue, and that young boy just doesn't seem to have a shred of it. I feel so ashamed to call him my nephew. I'm sure his Late father, my own brother, would've been ashamed of him too, if he was here. God rest his soul!

REV TRUMAN   Well, I prayed and fasted about the whole situation, as I said I would, and the Lord showed me a solution. The direction is that we must go to see Dennis, in person, and appeal to him – just the three of us. He will listen this time.

VIOLA   You mean for us to go to *Paradise Estate*?

REV TRUMAN   Well, if that's how we can face him and appeal to him, then we have to make an exception and go to *Paradise Estate*. Because from what I'm hearing, we only have one day left to make this journey, before the planned *Mongoose* and *Possum* gang-clash, as well as a separate planned revolution, involving people from all over the island.

VIOLA   *(astonished, makes the sign of the cross)* God forbid!

REV TRUMAN   I tell you, it'll be pandemonium and bloodshed on our streets. This was confirmed by a dream or maybe a vision, in my sleep. I saw

	fire and bloodshed on the streets, when I was on the last day of my fasting. And Brethren, my spirit tells me we must hurry, eh! Time is not on our side! *(there's very loud knocking on the door)*
ASHLEY	*(opens the front door to a bleeding man)* Oh my God! What happen to you man?
MR. BRIGHT	*(delirious, bawls uncontrollably)* Help me! They pour acid on me; I can't see. All-you help me! Please, help me! They killing me! *(fainting, slumps to the ground)*
ASHLEY	*(shouting in panic)* Viola! Reverend! All-you come quick! Bring a towel!
VIOLA	*(with towel gasps)* Lord have mercy! It's Mr Bright – you know, the kidnapped politician.
REV. TRUMAN	How he get here? *(whispering)* Ashley, he dead?
ASHLEY	Someone must've brought him to our front door and run off. I looked but didn't see anyone. *(checks the man's pulse)* No, he's not dead; but on death's door, though. Right now, I think he's unconscious because he's still breathing. Let's fan him. Viola, hand me that piece o' paper over there.
REV TRUMAN	*(trembling, prays)* The Lawd is my shepherd..... *(crying)*.....we shall not want...*(sniffling cries)* He makes us to lie down in green pastures. *(loudly, blows his nose)*
VIOLA	*(tending to his wounds)* Look how they mash-up this poor man! It's a wonder he still breathing or actually made it here, alive!

3:4   PAPA BOIS: KING OF PARADISE

MR BRIGHT	*(regaining consciousness)* Water! Water! Ow, that hurts! I beg you, please don't kill me! *(faints again)*
ASHLEY	*(offering water, speaks loudly)* Mr Bright, can you hear me? You'll be alright! Just hold on! We gonna take care of you, just stay with us!
RADIO	*(radio in the background)* "BREAKING NEWS! We interrupt this program to bring you Capital Radio's breaking news this hour."
ASHLEY	Quick-quick V, turn up the volume! Let's hear what's going on.
RADIO	*(music stops abruptly)* "This is Tom Cruz for Capital Radio 106 FM. News has just come in, about an outbreak of severe fighting on various streets in and around the capital, this morning. Since then, several areas have reported outbreaks of violence, rioting, looting and gun shots. We're told many have been injured, but there's no news of fatalities as yet. Let's go over live to Government house, for their immediate reaction to this developing situation, which by all accounts, appear to be spreading from area to area, around the island."
GOVERNMENT SPOKESMAN	"My fellow country men and women, this is Governor Richardson. I appeal to you <u>all</u> for calm, at this time. There's no need to take the law into your own hands, whatever your grievances. Please, remain in your homes, stay off the streets, and stop the violence! If the situation persists, we'll have no option but to initiate immediate curfew or complete lockdown, and bring the perpetrators to

	justice at once! As I speak, law enforcement officers are being deployed to your areas, to quell the situation and restore peace and order amongst you. That's all for now, you'll be apprised of the situation as things develop, but for now, PLEASE STAY IN YOUR HOMES, STAY OFF THE STREETS AND STOP THE VIOLENCE!"
RADIO	"So you've all heard it from the Governor. We're standing by for further updates, and rest assured, we're with the Government on this; STAY CALM PEOPLE! Until our next bulletin, this is Tom Cruz for Capital Radio 106 FM." *(music returns)*
REV TRUMAN	*(very solemn)* Lawd, the mayhem has started. That's what I was afraid of, my vision of bloodshed on our streets.
ASHLEY	So what go we do now? What can *anybody* do now? It's not safe to go out there!
MR BRIGHT	*(regains consciousness again, but is delirious)* Stop punching me! Ow! That kick broke my nose! Now you stepping on my head, Oh God! Aaai! *(crying, then vomits)*
VIOLA	*(shaking her head, whispers)* That's what they did to him? *(makes the sign of the cross).* Lawd have mercy! *(shocked, she covers her mouth with her hand)*
ASHLEY	V., quickly, bring more towel and a cushion to elevate his head.
VIOLA	*(consoles as she attends to him)* Hi, Mr. Bright, it's OK, you're safe now, you're here with us now. Look, there's my husband Ashley, Rev Truman and me, Miss V.

3:4   PAPA BOIS: KING OF PARADISE

	Remember us? Please calm down, we're trying to help you.
MR BRIGHT	*(continuing delirium)* Oh! They put acid in my eye! *(attempts to get up, enraged)* Help! Help! Somebody help me! I can't see. *(faints again)*
ASHLEY	*(shocked, clasps his hands)* Well, look what we've come too, and what for - Ganga, marijuana, cannabis, cocaine? *(shaking his head from side to side, remarks sternly)* This has got to stop now; one way or the other!
REV TRUMAN	*(looking skywards prays)* Father Gawd, as you can see, this madness is getting out of hand. We need you to intervene now!
ASHLEY/VIOLA	Amen!

[Curtains]

ACT 3 SCENE 5 - *"THE BEST LAID SCHEMES..."*

At Sam's Barber Shop, there's a discussion, in the aftermath of the 2-day rioting and looting. There's a planned surprise party and more trouble for Paradise Estate.

BARBER 1   You know, how glad I am, to be openin' up dis shop today, because havin' to close down dis little, strugglin' business, even for one day, is just too much for its survival, let alone 2 whole days. How we go pay de rent, if we doh open to make money?

BARBER 2   Well, let's just say we're lucky they didn't mash up the place or loot it; that would've been worse. Somehow we'll manage but the bigger problem is, ah think this whole two days of riotin' in the streets isn't the end of the matter, and so the worst is probably yet to come.

BARBER 1   Oh Gawd. Man, why you sayin' dat for?

BARBER 2   Well, ah hear *Mongoose* and *Possum* gangs still plannin' to battle it out again, after the curfew. So only God knows when all this stupidness goin' to stop?

BARBER 1   Listen eh, tell me somethin', such a little country as dis, and all dis *mele* going on, and for what? Look at dis Barber Shop, we doh have nice furniture or modern t'ings, but at least we're contented; we're doin' an honest trade!

BARBER 2   You're right! And who was it, who came all the way here, from America, with all their big highfalutin plans to drug-up we own country,

	and make our youngsters go mental, high on Ganga every day, and offering bribes, to keep them silent and stupid?
BARBER 1	Ah hear you, man! They say dis Dennis even givin' some of dem free food, free place to stay on de estate, and free drugs to keep dem high and obedient. And dat's not all, ah hear a lot of big, grown-ass men and women; some naked, and drunk, are runnin' around de place, like a drugged-up mental asylum!
BARBER 2	Eh-eh! What a wicked and evil man! *(lowers voice)* And between you and me, the worst is, ah hear some young people even died from drugs overdose and they bury them right on the estate, to avoid publicity.
BARBER 1	What! *(spits out a curse)* Pli maliwal! De devil done take dat evil Dennis soul. *(curses again)* Pli maliwal!
BARBER 2	Well, Reggie, who's comin' here for a trim shortly, told me about some of the goings-on at that drug and sex paradise. It seems all kind ah nasty, high-level criminals comin' into this country daily and freely, to openly trade in marijuana, take part in sex orgies, drunkenness, unstoppable flow of alcohol, spreading sexual diseases all over the place, and at the same time, givin' our country a real bad name?
BARBER 1	And to make matters worse, hundreds of people injured in de last riot, ah hear 5 young people died, and Gawd knows how many more is *not counted* for in de newspaper

	total, because they're too scared to come forward!
BARBER 2	One t'ing though, ah know a lot more people angry now, because Dennis is still untouched, nobody punished him, and he's thrivin' better than before! In fact, with the extra publicity in the news, if anythin', he seem to have licence to flaunt the laws, even more. *(whispers)* And speakin' of the devils, here comes Reggie.
REGGIE	*(enters jovially, rubbing his hands)* Marning! Marning! Howdy-do!
BARBER 1	Wha' happenin' dey, Reggie?
REGGIE	Well, all's good; ah really can't complain.
BARBER 2	So, you young people riotin', mashin' up the place, killin' youngsters, causin' mayhem everywhere for all kinda people and you standin' there sayin', *all's good*, you *can't complain*! What kinda stupidness is this?
REGGIE	Hey, don't take it out on me, man! I'm not Dennis Palmer, I don't own *Paradise Estate*. And furthermore, did he get punish for anythin'?
BARBER 1	And why didn't they? How come nobody close down dat drug-tradin' den of iniquity?
REGGIE	It's like ah said, many times before, Dennis is a very, very, smart businessman. He keeps everyone he's dealin' with sweetly bribed, and they're all happy to look the other way. You know, times are rough, and a little back-pocket-full-of-money type of help, just seems to do the trick for Dennis!
BARBERS	*(silent exchange of disapproving looks)*

3:5   PAPA BOIS: KING OF PARADISE

BARBER 2   Well, Mr. Kingpin Mikey, your hair-cut session starts now. *(points to the empty chair)* Come, sit down here!

REGGIE   *(sits in the barber chair)* Give me a No. 2 cut today, eh. Not too low, and can you make it quick. Have some errands to run before tonight's big bash.

BARBER 1   So what's with dis big bash? Wha' happenin' down there tonight?

REGGIE   *(jovial mood)* Well, *(looks cautiously around),* I guess I don't mind tellin' all-you. We goin' to have some real high profile Barons from Latin America, tonight. In fact, they're goin' to meet with some of our government officials at *Paradise Estate* tonight.

BARBER 1   So, you sayin' they goin' to be partyin' down there?

REGGIE   Yes man, a real big party is planned, and as far as I know, *EVERYTHING* is free: food, drugs, men, women, hotel apartments, money, alcohol; as we say, it's goin' to have a lot of wine, women, and song! That's why ah want a good hair-cut, because that last bit, 'wine women and song,' is my cue!

BARBER 2   Oh, is so? That's what all-you goin' to do down there? *(jokingly)* Suppose ah cut your neck with me shavin' blade right now! *(Reggie jumps up from the Barber's chair)*

BARBER 1   *(panicking gestures with his outstretched hands)* Alright, alright, don't sin yourself, man. You heard him say he's not Dennis

3:5 PAPA BOIS: KING OF PARADISE

Palmer, and he's right; cuttin' any part of him right now is not goin' to solve anythin'.

REGGIE *(worriedly defending)* Yes, and you should know you shouldn't shoot the messenger; all ah want is a hair-cut, to look good; not a neck-cut!

BARBER 2 *(laughing)* OK, don't get so pectus. All-you can't take a joke? Ah just messin' with you, man. But seriously though, while all-you makin' your illegal big bucks in a one-night deal on *Paradise Estate*, ah have to work me backside off, day-in and day-out, tryin' to earn pennies. *(shrugging)* But, hey man! That's not your problem, right! Come back here and sit down, man, let me cut your hair!

BARBER 1 And you say, *everyone's* invited to dis big bash in *Paradise* tonight?

REGGIE Yeah man, all who-is-who in government goin' to be there too. Let's just say that *Paradise* is celebratin' its superior position in the country: *(gestures with hands) untouchable, unstoppable, unbreakable*! At least that's what the boss said, and you know, Dennis Palmer is the *King of Paradise*; so he's always right!

BARBER 2 *(showing him the mirror)* OK, ah finish now; you look good for tonight!

REGGIE *(pays him)* Thanks a lot, eh. *(smiling happily)* With all those women, alcohol and special sinsemilla, planned for tonight, *(jokes)* I hope ah go live to tell all-you about it, next time we meet. *(laughs loudly)*. Is joke ah

3:5   PAPA BOIS: KING OF PARADISE

makin', eh; but ah have to go now, *(jovially his fist touches his chest)* One love!
[Exits]

BARBER 1   *(via clenched teeth)* Dat scrap of a boy, have a lot of nerve comin' here and boastin' about dat sinful Sodom and Gomorrah, he calls *Paradise*. He needs a good slap behind 'e head!

BARBER 2   Doh mind him, man. Idiots like that never get ahead, they just livin' hand-to-mouth; and for one day at a time.

MIKEY   *(enters the shop)* Morning, Brothers, I can see I doh have to ask how you managed with de riots, because dey didn't loot your place. And dat's a blessin'!

BARBER 1   You mean a temporary reprieve!

MIKEY   What you mean?

BARBER 1   Well, a little bird just told us some news dat you need to hear about.

MIKEY   Eh-heh! Go on, then!

BARBER 1   So, it seems like de government's in bed with some nasty Drug-Lords who're comin' into de country from South America tonight; maybe they're here already. These bed-fellows are notorious global drug-traders and they'll be at *Paradise* tonight.

MIKEY   *(shaking his head thoughtfully)* I see!

BARBER 2   Ah think what he's tryin' to say is, if anybody *really* wanted to upset *Paradise* little mango-cart, then tonight would be the time to do it! And you didn't just hear that from me, right!

MIKEY   I get your drift brothers! *(thoughtfully)* So they plan to clinch some big drug deals, right

	under our noses, actin' as if we damn stupid! Didn't we just riot recently? Like dey playin' a game with us, or what!
BARBER 1	Now, ah don't know how easy it would be to get inside *Paradise Estate* tonight, but ah get de feelin' dat a lot of people are invited, with everythin' goin' free; drugs, alcohol, women, men, hotel apartments, and food, would be a good time to pay dem a little visit.
MIKEY	So you say tonight's goin' to be one big drunken orgy, den!
BARBER 2	Ah definitely sayin' so. *(moving closer to whisper)* And ah guess not *everyone* will be on-guard, as they should be. *(winking)* You get my drift?
MIKEY	Yeah, ah get you, man!
BARBER 1	*(looking skywards and pointing)* And tonight's a full moon too. *(wildly flashing his teeth with widened eyes).* Ah when it's de full moon, you know what they say, de time's ripe for craziness! *(half-serious laughs)* A full moon mean de goddess Lunar, will be comin' down to sprinkle her lunatic dust on wicked humans; *La Diablese* will be busy streakin' across de skies in search of blood for *Basil-the-Devil*; *Papa Bois* will become a werewolf for one night, to transform de fortunes of de wicked. Insanity will be de order of de night, as duppies and men exchange personalities in mischievous behaviour. *(appeals to Mikey)* My friend, ah tellin' you, tonight will be a good time to strike!

3:5   PAPA BOIS: KING OF PARADISE

MIKEY   **[Aside]:** Den *tonight* is de night! *(jumps up impatiently)* Listen eh, let me take my haircut another time, instead of today, because ah have to go somewhere right now. *(whispers)* Ah need to ground with de brothers real fast, to prepare a big surprise tonight, for de *King of Paradise* and his special guests!

BARBER 1 We'll be right here when you're ready, man! Look around, do we look as if we're goin' anywhere? *(chuckles)*

MIKEY   *(sighing, with a self-satisfied smile)* Alright, brothers, we go catch up!

BARBER 2 Walk good eh, you don't need *luck*, because we're right behind you in spirit. *Papa Bois* will be there with you, and as for *Papa Gawd*; man, he'll surely be there on your side too.

[Curtains]

ACT 3 SCENE 6: ... *GO OFT AWRY, AND LEAVE US ONLY GRIEF AND PAIN"*

It is almost midnight, men have gathered in strategic locations, not far from the perimeter of Paradise Estate. Some armed men and women are led by Azacca from the north, others by Noah from the south, and another group by Leslie, from the east of the country; all waiting for the order from Mikey, to descend on Paradise Estate. In the meantime, Dennis Palmer, King of Paradise, and his minions in a sexual orgy, are entertaining drug Barons, specially invited government officials, tourists, other local and international clients.

Outside of Paradise Mansion, in the dark night, battle plans are secretly being finalised

MIKEY *(in a controlled low tone)* Now, tonight's what we've been waitin' for; to get rid of de cancer dat's spreadin' in our country. Remember why you're here. It's not de time to feel sorry for anyone. It's now or never! Now all-you from de North will follow Azacca; those from de south will follow Noah. We enterin' de Estate from de side entrance. Wait for my order to "charge" and we'll take down everythin' and everyone in sight.

NOAH *(in a controlled low tone)* Well, de good news is, *Paradise* security have let their guard down. Dere seems to be no security on de back side, so our group already doused de entire perimeter with gas. Every propagator will be ignited by small groups of 6 people, to make sure dey burn everythin' to de ground. With de fire spreadin' from de back, 3 other groups responsible for settin' fire all around de other areas, will torch de place at de same time. Any resistance will be dealt with by *Mongoose gang;* they're going to fight alongside us, and have guns to provide de firepower back-up we'll need.

LESLIE *(in a controlled low tone)* As for me and my group, some of us will mingle inside and pretend to be guests, so we infiltratin' from de inside also. Some will be located in de basement packagin' area. A few will be inside de apartment rooms, with gas-bottles nearby to ignite dem. We have an inside man, someone called Mark, operatin' inside their *Possum Gang*, who told us where de main power-switch is. So de plan is, all lights servicin' de entire estate will go off at once; dat's in exactly an hour's time. *(sniggers)* De big joke is, dey really believe Mark is one of dem, and payin' him to give dem information on us! Once de power goes off, dat will disable all de electrical fences, so everyone can charge in, without being electrocuted. At de same time, everyone inside will be trapped in de dark!

MIKEY *(in a controlled low tone)* OK, so take up your cutlass, machetes, bull-pistols, swords, hammers, hack-saws, axes, spears, sticks, guns, and gasoline; we go burn down *Paradise* to ashes tonight. And to make our

	job easy, no ambulance, police or fire truck will gain access to dis place, because ah understand dat for some reason, dis problem's already been taken care of! Ah hear de main road entrance to de Estate gate, is over-run with animals, and nobody seems to know whe' they come from.
NOAH	*(in a whisper)* It must be *Papa Bois*, man! Somebody say around 10 o'clock, dey hear a horn blowin' and from nowhere, all kinda animals appeared grazin', and de reason why I say is *Papa Bois*, someone say dey saw an old man with de animals; like he looking after dem! De good news is, de animals won't be harmed, because dey're half a mile near de main road, away from here. De better news is, no transport, no matter how hard dey try, will be able to gain access to dis place to help *Paradise* tonight.
MIKEY	*(in a controlled low tone)* Remember, dis mission's to burn down everythin' to de ground; not one pole must be left standin'. And if people have to be trapped in de process, den so be it, we go cleanse we own country of de evil. Make sure all-you do de job completely. *(Pauses)* So, now all-you know what you have to do, if anybody want out, now is de time to do it. Leave, if you doh have de guts for what we goin' to do now!
NOAH	*(holds a hand up in the pause and looks around)* OK, your silence means we're all in.

3:6   PAPA BOIS: KING OF PARADISE

MIKEY   Brothers, and sisters, we takin' back our land and our country dat allowed a disease to grow and fester right here, on dis west side, like an infestation. So, like cockroaches, if you are being over-run by dem, you have to exterminate de unwanted pests. *(hold his fist in the air chanting)* Babylon must fall! Long live de revo!

ALL   Long live de revo!

MIKEY   *(in a controlled low tone)* Yes, long live our revolution! Follow your group leader's order and wait for de final 'Charge'. Dis time tomorrow will be a new day, a new way, a new land. *(armed with various weapons, all stealthily disperse into the dark)*

[Exit]

ACT 3 SCENE 7 – *AS IT WAS IN THE BEGINNING......*

Inside Paradise Mansion Ballroom, Latin-American music is being played, with low level talking in Spanish, merrymaking, and excessive indulgence of all kinds; are in progress.

DENNIS	*(conversation with a Drug Baron is taking place in a corner of the ballroom)* OK Filippo, we counted last night's shipment; 2,000 pieces of AK-47s right? I must say, with merchandise like that on a weekly basis, we'll have a real good relationship. *(Smiles and shakes Filippo's hand, motions across the room)* Now, Adam over there, will take you upstairs to Santino, who will count the cash and hand it over to you.
FELIPPO	*(pulls out a cigar and lights it)* As long as we can do business like that, without competition, *(puffs on his cigar, staring directly at Dennis.* And since your place is open, to clean-up our dirty money, man, we have a flipping, good deal! *(puffing, blows smoke in the air)*
DENNIS	*(rubbing his hands together, looks around the room, then raises his voice over the music)* Well, gentlemen, now that tonight's real business is over, don't leave a single glass empty for more than a minute! Fill them up! Drink! Dance! Let's Par-tee! *(loudly, he points to naked women dancers)* Hey! Guys, these gals not to your liking? Then why are they still on the dance floor? Compadres! Enjoy yourselves, you're in *Paradise*! There

3:7   PAPA BOIS: KING OF PARADISE

	are over 50 rooms on the floors above us, to pleasure yourselves. *(waves his hand)* Go on, take them to your rooms and have fun! Vamoose!
VISITOR 1	*(heavy accented Latino speaker)* Bueno, as for me, I'm taking this little cherry upstairs; it's just ripe for the picking. *(touches a shy pre-teenage, young girl)* Come with papa!

[Exit]

VISITOR 2   *(whispers to Dennis)* Compadres, if this big fat sample is a taste of what I ordered, then let's just say, you have a deal for life man: *(motions with his hands)*, today, tomorrow, and the day after that, and so on and so on! *(unsteady on his feet, he leans across and deeply inhales cocaine from a woman's cleavage)* Come! It's time for fun! The night is still young, let's go upstairs! *(she props him up as they leave the room).*

[Exit]

DENNIS   *(speaking loudly)* Oh, come on DJ! Is this a funeral or what? Turn the music up! *(looks at his Rolex watch)* It's only midnight, let's make some noise in this place! Where are my pole dancers?

BIG T   *(rushing to his side)* Boss, every girl is taken by the other guests, for the night. *(thinks quickly)* But I can bring some packers up from the basement; *(mutters under his breath)* They won't need to change, they're already naked! *(sniggers)*

DENNIS   *(patting him on the back)* Then, what you waiting for, Big T? Go get them!

3:7   PAPA BOIS: KING OF PARADISE

BIG T Yes boss, right away!
  [Exit]

DENNIS *(intoxicated, he walks around looking smug)* Yes, the night is young, AND EVERYTHING TONIGHT IS FREE AND EASY - food, women, men, wine, alcohol, and the best that my *Paradise* can produce, on this side of the globe. *(calls out to a Buyer who's lighting a cigar)* Isn't that so, Juan?

JUAN *(A bodyguard translates Juan's reply)* Es el major del mundo! *(pointing to his body guard)* Por favor traduzcalo!

BODYGUARD *(gesturing a thumbs-up)* He says your product is, 'the best he's ever had!'

DENNIS *(walks towards Stacey)* Stace, you hear that?

STACEY *(dressed in a long red laced dress, like a brothel Madame)* Yeah, I heard him, Hon!

DENNIS *(laughing, approaches Stacey)* Then, long may *I*, Dennis, *King of Paradise,* reign with you as my *queen*! *(intoxicated, with out-stretched hand, bows but almost falls over)* My queen, what do you say we go upstairs too, eh? *(boasting, kisses her neck)* Tonight Stace, is our finest yet, in *Paradise!*
  [Exit]

*All lights throughout Paradise Estate go off. Gun shots, noises, scuffling, shouting, fighting, angry voices can be heard, as men burst into the rooms at Paradise. Charging, they ransack the place. **ENTER** Reggie with some men holding flash-lights and weapons, finds Dennis and Stacey naked in bed, in the master bedroom.*

3:7   PAPA BOIS: KING OF PARADISE

MIKEY Well, well, well! Look who's hidin' in here! *(shines a torch in Dennis' face, guns are pointed at both Dennis and Stacey in bed)*

AZACCA *(excitedly, points a gun at Dennis)* Rhaatid! See him dey. Him just a likky-likky bwoy cum to tief from us and kill us in de process. Wah di rass you hiding in here for? I'an'I go bump off you rassclaat, right now!

DENNIS *(naked, both hands up, begs)* Look fellas, *(eyeing his gun on the table next to the bed)* I don't know what you want but...

MIKEY *(interrupts and points a second gun at Dennis)* No buts! And doh even think about dat gun you starin' at, on de table over there. Eh-eh, so you really think you is a *king*! D'you *really* want to know what we want? *(audibly, he cocks the gun)*

STACEY *(both hands up, screams)* Please! Please don't do this! Don't hurt us - please, I'm begging you! *(sobs loudly)*

AZACCA *(points his gun now at Stacey)* Shut up Babylon, or I'n'I go blast you bombaclaat!

MIKEY Let me school them first before you blow their brains out. All-you people who come to dis country, some of you left us and couldn't even wait to leave dis land to stay away for donkey's years. So know, you not a local. All-you left because you either couldn't deal with dis place, too weak or too damn *caca poule* and worthless. We, de locals who stayed behind, gettin' our $35 and $60US an hour, diggin' a drain or pickin' coconut, we have to make our shit happen. We don't

ITRAN have your luxury, so you cyan know what it's like to be livin' in dis island.
You shoulda keep your backside quiet in America, instead of comin' here. But noh, you behavin' like you is Jesus Christ. Den dress up with your fancy clothes, you come here to show off with your kiss-me-ass evil business! When all-you go foreign and make there your own home, it's we, de locals, who have to decide everythin' what you foreign-based people don't know about.

DENNIS *(hands still held up)* Look, I know everyone is really angry right now, but please, I beg you, just put the gun down and let's talk. Sure we can sort this out. Nobody has to die, man.

MIKEY *(shouts angrily, pointing his gun at Dennis)* Well, now, isn't he the *Beggin' King of Paradise*! Just look at him! De cancerous evil dat spread and kill so many of our young people and ruin so many families throughout dis land, is now beggin' for his life! *(sneering)* You damaged generations for life; do you know how many died in riots because of you? And to make matters worse, you have our government officers under your evil spell too; wilfully breakin' our laws. *(gun still pointing, moves closer to Dennis and Stacey)* Well, I'd say *you* **have to** die!

DENNIS *(both hands up)* Guys! Guys! I get you. Let's talk, please. Put the gun down, so we can sort this out.

MIKEY Well, look at Dennis Palmer, who calls himself *king,* now you want to talk? *(scoffs)*

3:7 PAPA BOIS: KING OF PARADISE

You come here, all de way from America, with your big, crazy ideas: buildin' big, big drug enterprise, in our little country, and deliberately creatin' drug addiction habits for innocent lives among our youngsters. *(stamps his foot)* Man, dat's generations you ruined!!

ITRAN Yeah, you tell him! They come here with their hoity-toity self to show off on us. Right now we go curse all-you ass off good; before we kill you. Hear me, when I say whether is you or your parents, you're no longer citizens in dis island. Because all-you give up your citizenship here when you left and gone, and swear under oath to become foreign citizens somewhere else. All you turn your back, den all-you sit down and eat your big food; bacon, eggs, and ham and livin' your big life. We, on de other hand, eatin' we 2 figs. Still, we have our dignity; you wouldn't know what it means to be livin' in dis island. So, haul all-you ass! Mikey, doh waste any more time, man; just pull de damn trigger now!

STACEY *(sobbing, both hands up)* Please, please, don't do it! Don't shoot us! I beg you!

MIKEY Now, de two of you damn-well know our youngsters would always have to depend on your evil products to prop up their mashed-up, addicted lives. You infiltrated communities, from parish to parish, and ruined our country's name! And now you want to talk quietly! *(shakes his head)* Ah-ah! Not now! No way! No how!

3:7   PAPA BOIS: KING OF PARADISE

DENNIS *(both hands up, pleading)* Look guys, I know everyone's really angry right now, but we can still work something out. Just ask me for anything you want. Please, I can give you whatever you want. ANYTHING - just name it! *(voice becoming louder)* But whatever you do, please don't pull that trigger!

MIKEY Tell me *King Dennis*; did you just bribe me? *(angrier, a gun at Dennis' head)*; All-you hear that, right? Even as dis cockroach is on his last leg, he t'ink his dirty money can still buy him favours!

AZACCA *(also points his gun at Dennis)* Dat likky-likky bwoy, im too feisty! I'n'I ready to blast his bombaclaat to hell right now; just say de word!

DENNIS *(still pleading, both hands up)* Look, I'm not trying to bribe anyone; please, I'm just asking you to put the gun down and let's work this out, nobody has to get hurt or die!

MIKEY *(still pointing a gun at close range at Dennis' head)* Shut up, you mass murderer! You doh know what de word *hurt* means. You're one man, who took many lives, broke families' hearts, and still have de nerve to say, *(mimics Dennis)* "Please don't kill us!" *(cocks the gun)* Well, Dennis Palmer, you'll now feel what *hurt* really is. *(visibly agitated, breathing heavily, he moves closer, clicks his gun, voice raises to a yell)* TONIGHT, DENNIS PALMER, IS YOUR LAST NIGHT IN YOUR PARADISE! *(screams from Stacey as he pulls the trigger, shoots Dennis, then shoots her)*

3:7   PAPA BOIS: KING OF PARADISE

AZACCA   (*triumphantly*) Yes! dis place im have here, is NOT, and could NEVA BE Paradise for I'an'I. (*defiantly holds fist up in the air*) Jah! Rastafari!

MIKEY   (*scorns the bodies, turns to those around him*) Now all-you know what to do - burn everythin' down to de ground!

There is scrambling and confusion everywhere, as gun-shots are heard, sounds of screaming, bawling, and wailing are interspersed with calls of "charge!" as fire engulfs from one estate building to the other. Doors are locked with the drunken and the drugged inside, too high to save themselves, as attackers rummage the Estate. The violent battle rages on in Paradise, from the early hours of the morning, until daylight, and the vast estate space resembles the scene after a nuclear fall-out. An eerie silence pervades the empty space, now enveloped with thick grey smoke rising to the sky; as everything in sight is reduced to ashes.

[Curtains]

EPILOGUE   PAPA BOIS: KING OF PARADISE

EPILOGUE

A decade after the demise of Paradise Estate, Canadian Eco-tourists, Patrick and Ella, are preparing for their Paradise Nature Reserve Tour. Whilst waiting for their Tour Guide, whom they met the night before, they look around a Gift Shop, surveying various memorabilia and souvenirs of the Nature Reserve. However, they are perplexed and shocked by a very strange discovery.

ELLA *(to Patrick)* Look, I bought this book, *Birdwatchers* – it's supposed to catalogue the hidden birdlife in this Reserve that's not found anywhere in the world. According to this book, we may even get to listen to some of them.

PATRICK Now, if we could see some and hear them too, that would be nice! Look, this one's nice, it caught my eye because it says the writer makes a connection between nature's positive effects on the brain. *(opening his shopping bag)* Then there's this one too, *The Natural Health Science* - about the remedies found in this *Reserve*: it has 200 hand-drawn illustrations and 50 colour photographs of the species and plants that influence mental well-being.

ELLA Yes, they both look good. I'd love to read them when you're done. Er, I did promise myself to buy two books also, and the other one I saw is over there. I'll get it now, then we should be ready to set off for today's tour.

EPILOGUE — PAPA BOIS: KING OF PARADISE

PATRICK: OK, I'll be right here, having a peek at my little goodies.

ELLA: *(shouts loudly)* Patrick! Patrick, you've got to come and see this. *(raised voice)* Come quickly!

PATRICK: *(leaves his corner of the Gift Shop walks over to Ella)* Something the matter?

ELLA: *(seems shocked, hand covering her mouth)* Look at this book, *"Paradise Nature Reserve or Garden of Eden?"*

PATRICK: OK, so what's wrong with it!

ELLA: *(Hands a book to Patrick).* Tell me I'm not dreaming! Open it, look inside!

PATRICK: *(impatiently whispers)* Alright honey, calm down. *(he opens the book)*

ELLA: *(stammering)* L-L-Look inside, Chapter 1, page 5, *"Secrets of the Reserve,"* what can you see?

PATRICK: *(puzzled, turns swiftly to Ella)* Why, it's ….. *(whispering in disbelief)* Moses? Isn't this the same person we laughed and talked with yesterday?

ELLA: *(surprised)* Well, yes, unless our eyes are deceiving us right now, that's what I can see. But… isn't this person in the book the same Tour Guide who told us the story of *Paradise Nature Reserve*, last night? *(hesitates, lowers voice)* He's not supposed to be a real person. Look, here in this book, he is called *Papa Bois* - a folktale character!

PATRICK: Well, according to the picture here in this book, the man who told us the story about *Paradise Nature Reserve*, in the Reception

EPILOGUE	PAPA BOIS: KING OF PARADISE
	yesterday, seems to be this same *Papa Bois*, here in the picture we're looking at now, and is not Moses!
ELLA	*(surprised, whispers)* This is giving me goose-pimples. Does that mean we spent the evening talking to a ghost last yesterday? The man we spent the evening drinking, chatting, and laughing with, told us his name was Moses, our Tour Guide for the Reserve. But according to this book, he is the legendary folktale *Papa Bois!*
PATRICK	*(overwhelmed)* Hang on, pay for your purchases and let's get some air; this is kinda freaking me out.
ELLA	*(attempts to sound upbeat)* Better still, let's go and find our Tour Guide, I'm sure this little enigma can be easily cleared up, you'll see!
PATRICK	*(walks to the Receptionist)* Hi, we've booked for the Nature Reserve Tour we'll be taking today. Is our Tour Guide here yet?
RECEPTIONIST	Yes, Sir. He's right over there behind you. His name's Moses.
PATRICK	*(turns around, looking puzzled)* Is *your* name Moses?
MOSES	Yes, I'm Moses, your Tour Guide. And who are you, sir? *(Looks at his clip-board for their names)*
PATRICK	*(dumb-founded)* Er...I'm Patrick and this is my wife Ella. Er... we've never met you before, have we? I mean...Er....is there another Moses amongst your Tour Guide team?

EPILOGUE   PAPA BOIS: KING OF PARADISE

MOSES *(staring at the two)* You're both looking a little confused right now, but no sir, there's no Tour Guide Team; there's only one Tour Guide, and that's me, Moses. Is something the matter?

ELLA *(trying to sound upbeat)* No-no! Don't worry, please, we're fine, really. We thought we'd met the Tour Guide last night. You know, had a drink, a chat and a laugh with him, but clearly it's not you. *(embarrassed, she laughs nervously)* Probably the heat, you know, the weather is very hot! *(whispers to Patrick)* This is not the Moses we met last night, and he just said there's only one Moses!

PATRICK *(Whispering)* I know. So, what's going on? *(he looks at Ella, shrugging his shoulders)* So, that means...?

ELLA *(quizzically)* Well... could it mean that we met *Papa Bois*, as the picture in the book shows, who pretended to be Moses, the Tour Guide, last night?

PATRICK Yeah, but my question is, how come? How is it possible, and why?

ELLA *(shaking her head, she shrugs her shoulders)* You know what, I too haven't a clue! This whole thing really beats me!!

[Curtains]

END OF PLAY

GLOSSARY OF TERMS

ACT 1 SCENE 1 – *WELCOME TO PARADISE!*

1. **Maroon** – A term derived from Spanish *Cimarron,* meaning 'wild or unruly', refers to slaves in various parts of the Caribbean who, during slavery, ran away from slave plantations to create their own groups and communities as a strategy of resistance. Historically, these independent groups lived on the periphery of slave societies and were particularly prevalent in Brazil, Suriname, and Jamaica. In the context of this play, it refers to the practice of maroon society, e.g. the communal activity in challenging situations. This is shown by their autonomy, group strength, independence, self-determination, and self reliance. In the Eastern Caribbean, a large gang of workmen would voluntarily join forces to either plough a person's gardens during the planting season or assist in the moving and re-building of a house.

2. *we'll be all ears* – (to be) all ears, is to be attentive, or listening very carefully

ACT 1 SCENE 2 – *THE BEST LAID SCHEMES*

1. **The American Dream** – The "American Dream" is a concept or set of beliefs that drive American citizens, as they work toward creating a life for themselves. The ethos, which includes the notions of individual rights, freedom, democracy, and equality is, arguably, centered around the belief that each individual has the right and freedom to seek prosperity and happiness, regardless of where or under what circumstances they were born. In other words the key element is the belief that through hard work and perseverance, anyone can rise to the top, becoming financially successful and socially upwardly

GLOSSARY — PAPA BOIS: KING OF PARADISE

mobile. In this Play, the Caribbean and Italian immigrants who went to the United States, looking for their bit of life, liberty, the pursuit of happiness, and material prosperity, can be seen as chasing their American Dream.

2. **all man, Jack, and their brother** – an informal expression meaning, absolutely everyone included.

3. **Make hay while the sun shines** - it means that you take advantage of the chance to do something while the conditions are good.

4. **Beat the iron while it's hot** – means to act on an opportunity promptly while favourable conditions exist; in case they go away.

ACT 1 SCENE 3 – *A SENSE OF BELONGING*

1. **Puncha Crema, ponche crema or ponche de crème** - is a crème-based liqueur, traditionally served during Christmas time, in the Caribbean.
2. **Buon Natale** – Merry Christmas
3. **Buon Anno** – Happy New Year
4. **Felice anno nuovo** – Happy New Year
5. **Altrettanto!** – and the same to you!

ACT 1 SCENE 4 – *DENNIS RISES!*

1. **¿Qué pasa?** - What's going on? Or What's up?

ACT 2 SCENE 2 – *'THEM-AND-US'*

1. **All ah we is one** – We are one people, no separate identity in the Caribbean

ACT 2 SCENE 3 - *GRAVE CONCERNS*

1. **Everything turn ole mass!** – chaos and confusion
2. **Massa day done** – (*Massa*) meaning the Salve Master), is the symbol of a bygone age, slavery. An expression used

GLOSSARY   PAPA BOIS: KING OF PARADISE

to reproach someone to remind them that colonial days are finished, and old privileges and oppression are no longer acceptable (from a Public lecture by Eric Williams 22 March 1961)

ACT 2 SCENE 4 – GANGSTERS AND GREEDY MEN
1. *a strap* – slang for a gun
2. **greasing palm** – bribing others for favours
3. **Homie** – slang for a very close friend, someone who's always there for you. The term suggests the highest form of respect to another individual, as this person will always have your back through thick and thin The word *"homie"* originally referred to someone from your home town.

ACT 2 SCENE 5 – SCHEMES GO AWRY
1. *gear* – general slang for unspecified named drugs e.g. cocaine, marijuana, etc.

ACT 3 SCENE 1 - *THE DILEMMA!*
1. **side-hustle** - A side hustle is a way to make money outside of your 9 to 5 job
2. *lazin' about* – being idle, doing nothing
3. **Look at meh ass cross, noh!** Or sometimes expressed as, **Look at meh crosses!** - an expression that suggests you are currently in a terrible situation.

ACT 3 SCENE 3 – *MASSA DAY DONE!*
1. *kunumoonoo!* Or *kunimunu!* – (Yoruba *Kunun, kuni*), meaning a stupid person who is easily deceived or taken advantage of; a simpleton.
2. *AZACCA: Brethren, Greetin's in the name of His Imperial Majesty, Emperor Haile Selassie, Jah Rastafari, who liveth and reigneth I'n'I itinually, ever faithful, ever sure.*

GLOSSARY   PAPA BOIS: KING OF PARADISE

I'n'I seh fiyah bun babylon kaaz dem eva dey tarment poor people.

TRANSLATED: Brothers and Sisters, I greet you in the name of His Imperial Majesty, Emperor Haile Selassie, our God who lives and reigns in the Rastafarian brothers and sisters continuously, faithfully, and sure. We say we denounce Babylon (the enemy), because every day he, (the enemy), torments poor people.

NOTE: This greeting portrays the belief that Ras Tafari Haile Selassie I, Emperor of Ethiopia, is the Biblical Messiah. Though not expressed in this Play, he is also referred to as the Conquering Lion of the Tribe of Judah. This is why the lion is seen as a powerful symbol by Rastafarians, and believers greet each other with their belief and solidarity in this truth.

3. *AZACCA: But hear noh, a lat a greedy betrayer 'tween us, jus' sittin pon dem backside saying Mi nuh hav nutten fi complain bout, mi life irie, but mek ah tell you sumthin', I'n'I come here to say, jus' like Bob Marley did, wi guh chase dem crazy ball head outta town - dat Dennis and hi Possum gang, who come to grow and sell hi genetically modified blodclart sinsemilla here.*

TRANSLATED: But listen, quite a lot of greedy betrayers are among us, just lazily hanging around, saying they have nothing to complain about because their life is good, but let me tell you something, we come here to say, just like Bob Marley did, [in his song], we're going to chase those crazy ball-heads out of our town – Dennis and his Possum gang, who's come here to grow and sell his blasted genetically modified Ganga here.

NOTE: However, the word "ball-head" originally meant, those who don't wear dread locks hair styles.

4. **AZACCA:** *Dat Dennis is nat a real fiyah man, and dat thin' he selling is not de healing herb we know. Jus' like everytime, *Babylon come to trick I'n'I wit him poison, so wen we turn fool-fool, den he tek over everythin'. But we haffi play fool fi ketch wise and trap him.*

   TRANSLATED: Dennis is not a genuine person who burns the *righteous fire* (which is Ganga, smoked for Rastafarian religious purposes) man, and his type of Ganga is not the genuine kind of healing herb that we know. Just as before, he's come In the usual way that the enemy does, to deceive us with his poison, and then when we become less vigilant, he takes everything from us. So we, (the Rastafarian brothers and sisters), have to pretend to be silly or disguise our knowledge, (play the role of a fool), and let those around us, (in this case, the enemy), believe they are smarter, in order for us to later outsmart them.

   NOTE: (1). The smoking of marijuana or Ganga, plays an important role in Rastafarians' life. It is considered a sacred ritual in Rasta culture. Referred to as, the "*holy Herb,*" marijuana is highly valued for its physical, psychological, and therapeutic powers.

   NOTE: (2).* "*Babylon*" is the Rastafarian word for the police, who are viewed by Rastafarians as part of a corrupt government system. "Babylon", which refers to the Biblical rebellion against God through the Tower of Babel, can also be used to describe any person or organization that oppresses the innocent; hence, Dennis' operations is equated with oppression.

5. **AZACCA:** *Mi nuh truss deh bredda deh, kaaz him a bag o wire. So, I'n'I and mi brethren standin' wit you. I'n'I waitin' to chase dat crazy ball head outta our yard. We go chase Dennis and de politicians outta village, outta town*

and outta our island. Say wen, I'n'I, and mi brethren from the north, wi ready on standby! Nuff respect. (salutes with a raised fist) Jah!

TRANSLATED: I don't trust Dennis Palmer, because he is a betrayer or sell-out. So we (my bethren and I), will stand in solidarity with you all. We (the Rastafarian brothers and sisters) are waiting to chase the ballhead enemies (Dennis and his Possum gang), out of our country. We're going to chase the politicians out of our villages, towns and country. Just tell us when and we, the Rastafarian brothers and sisters, who are from the north [of the country], are ready on standby. A lot of respect [for everyone here].

NOTE: Ending with the expression of Jah Rastafari, symbolises unity, which exists in all people, unified by "Jah Rastafari." The word "Jah" is shortened for Jevohah, confirms the oneness of Jah Rastafari, their "God", the Ethiopian Emperor Ras Tafari Haile Selassie I, in every person.

6. **"a wolf in sheep's clothing"** – someone who appears friendly but is really hostile.

ACT 3 SCENE 5

1. **Pli maliwell** - (Creole French or *patois*), means *'I put a bad curse on you!"*
2. **La Diablese** – (pronounced La-ja-bless), is a Devil woman, who roams around at night. She takes the form of a beautiful woman, personified as an old embittered woman, roaming around at night, luring unsuspecting men to their deaths.
3. **Basil the Devil** – is a demon who resides I the silk cotton tree. He has a pact with blood sucking Soucouyants or Vampires, to trade their victims' blood with him, in exchange for granting them evil powers.

GLOSSARY   PAPA BOIS: KING OF PARADISE

4. **Ground with the brothers** – interact, discuss, impart knowledge, enlighten

ACT 3 SCENE 6

1. **Caca poule** – (French Creole for chicken- shit, meaning rubbish)

2. **JUAN:** *(A bodyguard translates Juan's reply)* ***Es el major del mundo!*** *(pointing to his body guard)* ***Por favor traduzcalo!***
   TRANSLATED: It's the best in the world. Translate it [to him] please.

3. **EGBERT:** ***Shut up or I'n'I go blast you bombaclaat!***
   TRANSLATED: Shut up or we (meaning I, and my Rastafarian brothers and sisters), will blast you to f…..ing hell!

4. **AZACCA :** ***Rhaatid! See him dey. Him just a likky-Likky bwoy cum to tief from us and kill us in the process. Wah di rass you hiding in here for? I'an'I go bump off you rassclaat, right now!***

   TRANSLATED: Flipping hell! Look at him! He's just a little boy, who's come to steal from us and kill us in the process. What the hell you hiding in here for? We (I and my Rastafarian brothers and sisters), will f..ing kill you right now!

   NOTE: Feelings are running high and words like **rassclatt**, (similar to **bombaclaat** above), are very derogatory words; it means you are essentially calling someone a tampon, (a menstrual pad), equated with saying the **"F"** word in English countries.

GLOSSARY   PAPA BOIS: KING OF PARADISE

5. **AZACCA: *(triumphantly)* Yes! dis place im have here, is NOT, and could NEVA BE Paradise for I'an'I. *(defiantly holds fist up in the air)* Jah! Rastafari!**
TRANSLATED: Yes, this place here, is NOT, and could NEVER be Paradise for us; meaning, (me and my Rastafarian brothers and sisters).

Books by the Same Author:

- *Poems to Navigate Caribbean Diaspora Disruptions (2021)*
- *The Phantom of the Great House (2021)*
- *Gang-Gang Sarah: A Caribbean Sensation (2020)*
- *Shakespeare for Children: Macbeth (2020)*
- *11+ English Preparation Tests for the CEM Exam (2020)*
- *Phonics & Spelling Workbook 1 (2020)*
- *Rhythms of Life: An Anthology of Modern Poetry (2019*
- *Mastering Comprehension Skills (2019)*
- *The New Caribbean Folktales and Legends for the 21st Century (2018)*
- *English Grammar: A Student's Companion (2018)*
- *Vocabulary Skills for Students & Teachers: A Practical Learning Toolkit (2018)*
- *Spelling & Word Power Skills Volume 1 (2018)*
- *A Woman of Destiny: A Calypso Novel (2015)*
- *A Woman of Destiny: The Text Study Guide (2015)*
- *T A Marryshow CBE – Honouring Caribbean Greats (2001)*

Phoenix Study Guides published by Eagle Publications

www.eaglepublications.org.uk

www.ingramcontent.com/pod-product-compliance
Lightning Source LLC
Chambersburg PA
CBHW011958090526
44590CB00023B/3769